Prior to his call to the bar Duncan Craig had a nineteen-year career in the licensed trade. This started in 1991 when he worked in free trade sales for Whitbread for five years, followed by four years as a pub area manager for Eldridge Pope. He opened his first restaurant in Nottingham when he was still at Eldridge Pope and in 2000 focussed his efforts on building his own group of pubs, bars and restaurants which by 2006 comprised of six licensed premises in Nottingham employing over 120 people.

After losing that business in 2009 Duncan resolved to become a barrister and after completing the GDL and BPTC at Nottingham Law School he secured a pupillage at Citadel Chambers in Birmingham where he was a member for ten years during which time he built up a formidable licensing practice and became Head of Licensing. In 2023 Duncan moved to St Philips Chambers, also in Birmingham, which has a long-established reputation in the field of regulatory law. In 2025 Duncan became Deputy Head of the Regulatory Group at St Philips.

Duncan is widely regarded as the leading barrister in the field of licensing in the Midlands, one of the busiest licensing lawyers in the country and has conducted more expedited reviews than any other legal professional over the course of the last decade.

A Practical Guide to Summary Reviews Under the Licensing Act 2003

A Practical Guide to Summary Reviews Under the Licensing Act 2003

Duncan Craig, Barrister
St Philips Chambers, Birmingham

Law Brief Publishing

Published 2026 by Law Brief Publishing, an imprint of Law Brief Publishing Ltd
30 The Parks
Minehead
Somerset
TA24 8BT

www.lawbriefpublishing.com

Paperback: 978-1-918241-34-1

To Mike Jackson, my boss at Eldridge Pope from 1996 to 1999 where I was a pub area manager. Mike displayed a better instinct for the licensed trade than anyone I have encountered in the last 35 years, and I still find myself quoting his wise words to clients and colleagues alike on a regular basis.

PREFACE

Summary Reviews, or expedited reviews as they are sometimes known are a mechanism for swift regulatory intervention in relation to a premises that is licensed under the Licensing Act 2003 ('the Act') to sell alcohol, and where those premises have been found by a senior officer of the police service within which those particular premises are situated to be associated with serious crime. They are fast moving, for all parties involved, especially for the licence holder of the premises that is subject to the application to review their premises licence and can have profound consequences for their businesses in the short, medium and long-term, depending on the circumstances of the review and their response to it. However, as a creature of amended statute they operate in a highly structured, formulaic manner, and as the process continues licence holders can exercise a greater degree of control over proceedings than at the outset. These types of review applications often come out of nowhere as far as the licence holder is concerned, and frequently relate to premises that have had no particular issues with the police before, even in instances where those operators have owned those licensed premises for many years.

This book is directed towards all parties who can be part of this process: from police and local authority officers through to licence holders - and in particular the latter (and those who represent them) as they are likely to be much less familiar with the process than public sector officers whose involvement is vocational and therefore frequently more familiar. It is hoped that this book will provide a useful and purposeful pathway through a form of regulatory intervention which can be both distressing and overwhelming for those who are subject to summary reviews as well as providing guidance to other parties who are involved in the process.

The law quoted in this book was believed to be accurate as of 24th May 2026.

Duncan Craig
May 2026

GLOSSARY

Certificate: This commences the Summary Review process. It is signed by an officer of a police service in England and Wales of the rank of Superintendent or above and confirms the opinion of that officer that a particular licenced premises is associated with serious crime and/or disorder.

Committee Services: Sections within local authorities who are required to organise hearings (*inter alia*) under the Act and to distribute associated material to interested parties and attendees. Committee Services Managers are usually responsible for taking the minutes of any Summary Review hearings and often distribute the decision notice afterwards.

Conditions on a Premises Licence: These are restrictions or requirements that are placed on a Premises Licence relating to the operation of the business, and include the authorised hours for licensable activities. Some of these conditions are mandated by statute and others are specific to the particular premises. Breach of either can amount to a criminal offence.

Designated Premises Supervisor ('DPS'): The individual who authorises the sale of alcohol under a Premises Licence and this is the person who is supposed to have day-to-day control of the premises. A DPS must hold a personal licence, which are issued by Licensing Authorities in England and Wales.

Hearings Regulations (The Licensing Act 2003 (Hearings) Regulations 2005): Associated regulations that govern hearings under the Act, including in relation to Summary Reviews.

'Lalli'[1] Principal case law relating to Summary Reviews. The facts of this particular Summary Review related to a single incident of serious violence when a troublesome customer was forcibly ejected from a pub, including in which was being kicked in the region of his head in the process. There is no indication from the Judgment that this was anything but a one-off event. There had been no incidents of serious crime or disorder on the premises in the previous four years that the Claimant to the Judicial Review had held the licence. The case has established many of the key principles in Summary Reviews.

Licensing Authorities: Sections within local authorities that are responsible for administration, enforcement and decision making in relation to premises and personal licences as well as acting as a responsible authority under the Act. Many of their powers and responsibilities are enshrined in the Act.

Licencing Objectives: Four statutory objectives that licencing authorities are required by statute to promote when carrying out their functions under the Act. Those 4 licencing objectives are:

1. the prevention of crime and disorder;
2. the prevention of public nuisance;
3. public safety; and
4. the protection of children from harm

Licensable Activities: Activities that are authorised under and through a Premises Licence via the Act and are as follows

1. sale of alcohol by retail

---

[1] (R (Sharonjeet Lalli v Metropolitan Police Commissioner and Newham Borough Council [2015] EWCH 14 (Admin)

2. regulated entertainment

3. late night refreshment

Licencing Subcommittee: Panels of local councillors who convene to determine applications under the following hearings, including Summary Reviews. These are usually comprised of three councillors who are part of the council's licensing committee.[2]

Other Persons: Non-responsible authorities that can make representations to the Licensing Authority upon a Summary Review application. There used to be a vicinity test applied to these representations, but this was removed in 2012[3] so representations from any source are now valid as long as they are not frivolous, vexatious and are relevant to the Licensing Objectives.

Personal Licence: Issued by local authorities upon submission of an application accompanied by a certificate relating to a relevant qualification and a DBS certificate along with an application fee. A person cannot be a DPS without holding a valid personal licence.[4]

Premises licence: An authorisation under the Act to carry on licensable activities from a premises. A premises under the Act means any place and includes a vehicle, vessel or moveable structure.[5] A Premises Licence will have certain restrictions on it in relation to the hours that licensable activities are authorised and conditions that are placed upon it more widely.

---

2 Section 6(1) Licensing Act 2003

3 Section 115 Police Reform and Social Responsibility Act 2011

4 Section 19(2)(b) Licensing Act 2003

5 Section 193 Licensing Act 2003

Police Licensing Section: Sections within each police service which are dedicated to licensed premises and personal licences. As well as submitting review applications of both types and responding to premises and personal licence grant applications, they are also expected to interact with licensed premises on a proactive basis to promote the crime and disorder prevention Licensing Objective in particular. Police Licensing Sections also are often a useful source of intelligence to the wider police service within which they operate. They are often staffed by civilians as well as police officers.

Representation Period: The 10-working day period that responsible authorities and Other Persons have to make valid representations upon a Summary Review application, whether in support of the Review Application or the Licence Holder.[6]

Summary Review application: An application to review Premises Licence on behalf of the chief constable of a particular police service where in the opinion of a senior officer, those premises are associated with serious crime and/or disorder; although it is usually completed and submitted by a more junior officer or employee of that police service who works in the licencing function.

Section 182 Guidance: Published by the Home Office and updated periodically. The Section 182 Guidance ('the Guidance') provides guidance to licencing authorities in particular when determining applications under the Act and has a chapter dedicated to Summary Reviews (12). Licensing Authorities are required under the Act to have regard to the Guidance at all times when carrying out their functions under the Act.[7]

---

6 Regulation 39A(2) The Licensing Act 2003 (Premsies Licences and Club Premises Certificates) Regulation 2005

7 Section 4(3)(b) Licensing Act 2003

Statement of Licencing Policy: Each Licencing Authority is required to have a Statement of Licencing Policy which must be updated at least every five years.[8] It sets out that Licencing Authority's approach to the administration and enforcement of licencing under the Act within their area. Licensing Authorities are required under the Act to have regard to their own Statement of Licensing Policy at all times when carrying out their functions under the Act.[9]

Violent Crime Reduction Act 2006: Act of Parliament that brought Summary Reviews into force under the Act.

---

[8] Section 5(1) Licensing Act 2003

[9] Section 4(3)(a) Licensing Act 2003

CONTENTS

CHAPTER ONE

THE LICENSING ACT 2003

The Act was brought into force on the 24th November 2005. The Act fundamentally altered the way the licencing of premises was administered and enforced, and upon enactment it passed decision-making powers in licensing from Magistrates' Courts to local authorities in England and Wales. One of the key points of difference from the Licencing Act 1964 was it made the process of obtaining a licence to sell alcohol and perform live and recorded music more straightforward, but it also made the process of imposing changes upon such licences, and taking them away altogether, more straightforward.

The Act created responsible authorities, public bodies tasked with regulatory oversight into the licencing regime. Those responsible authorities are provided for in Subsection 13(2) of the Act and are (in straightforward terms)

- the relevant licensing authority in whose area the premises are situated;
- the chief officer of police for any police area in which the premises are situated;
- the fire and rescue authority for any area in which the premises are situated
- the Local Health Board for any area in which the premises are situated
- the local authority in England whose public health functions within the meaning of the National Health Service Act 2006 are

exercisable in respect of any area in which the premises are situated [public health]

- the enforcing authority within the meaning given by section 18 of the Health and Safety at Work etc. Act 1974 for any area in which the premises are situated [environmental health in respect of public safety]

- the local planning authority for any area in which the premises are situated

- the local authority by which statutory functions are exercisable in any area in which the premises are situated in relation to minimising or preventing the risk of pollution of the environment or of harm to human health [environmental health in respect of public nuisance]

- a body which represents those who, in relation to any such area, are responsible for, or interested in, matters relating to the protection of children from harm and is recognised by the licensing authority for that area for the purposes of this section as being competent to advise it on such matters [Trading Standards and the local Children Safeguarding Board, or equivalent].

- where the premises (not being a vessel) are being, or are proposed to be, used for a licensable activity within section 1(1)(a) or (d), the Secretary of State. [Immigration Enforcement]

Two responsible authorities are central to the Summary Review process.

i. **Licensing Authorities** perform a number of functions in relation to the Summary Review process. Firstly, they are required to administer the Summary Review once an application is made by the chief officer of police for the area within which the council is situated accompanied by the associated Certificate. This will include fixing the notice advertising the review application in a prominent place at the premises to which the application is subject. The Licensing Authority will also be required to liaise with Committee Services to organise any hearings, some of which will be required to be held at relatively short notice. Throughout the Representation Period the Licensing Authority will be required to receive and distribute any representations upon the Summary Review application to all relevant parties as well as any supporting evidence in support of any of those parties in relation to any hearings. The Licensing Authority will also be required to send out any decision notices in accordance with associated statutory time limits. The councillors who make any substantive decisions in relation to licensing applications are also, strictly speaking, part of the Licensing Authority.

ii. **Police Services** are the source of any and all Summary Reviews. It is enshrined within the Guidance that the police should be the 'main source of advice for licensing authorities' in relation to the prevention of crime and disorder Licensing Objective,[1] and this principle will always carry some weight, usually significant, with Licensing Subcommittees. This is an understandable and rational approach but sometimes means licensed premises face an uphill task in challenging the police's opinions or stance on their premises. Once the review application has been submitted along with the accompanying certificate signed by a senior officer, then short of that certificate being quashed there is nothing that can stop the Summary Review process taking its course.

---

1 Paragraph 9.12 Section 182 Guidance

Standard Reviews of Premises Licences

In order to understand a Summary Review, it is helpful to understand the mechanics and principles of a Standard Review of a Premises Licence, applied for under section 51, and determined under section 52 of the Act. Unlike Summary Reviews, which were introduced via Violent Crime Reduction Act 2006, Standard Reviews were part of the original body of the Act and have (apart from a few tweaks to the original wording) remained intact since November 2005.

A Standard Review of a Premises Licence is a process where someone, usually a responsible authority, is seeking some sort of change to a Premises Licence, or its revocation. This process is commenced by the completion of a review application form setting out the premises to which the application will be subject and the grounds for the review application, which is served upon the Licencing Authority within which those particular premises are situated.[2] It is usual for a Standard Review application to include within it what the applicant is seeking from the process, which can and frequently does include a request for revocation of the licence.

Standard Review applications commence a process that ends in a hearing (unless the parties can all agree it is not necessary) where the future shape and form of the licence under review is determined. The Standard Review process involves the advertising of the application, a requirement that the associated hearing is held within a certain period (in accordance with the Hearings Regulations)[3] and any decision that follows from the application can be appealed to the Magistrates' Court. The Standard Review process also invites representations from both responsible

---

2 Schedule 8 Licensing Act 2003 (Premises Licences and Club Premises Certificates) Regulations 2005

3 Paragraph 7 Schedule 1 Licensing Act 2003 (Hearings) Regulations 2005

authorities and 'Other Persons',[4] which if deemed relevant in the case of the latter, will make them parties to the Standard Review and entitled to attend the hearing.

After the Act was brought into force in November 2005 it quickly became apparent that there were significant limits to the Standard Review process which meant that licensed premises that were associated with serious crime (and in some instances involving fatalities) would not be subject to any immediate, effective and meaningful regulatory intervention, in that the hearing would take place some two months after the review application was submitted and any decision made by the Licensing Subcommittee at that hearing, if appealed, would not take effect until the determination of that appeal,[5] which could be many months after the hearing. This meant there was no lawful power under the Act to prevent badly run and dangerous premises from carrying on as before for several months after a serious incident.

This meant that consideration was given to ways of addressing this by amending the Act by inserting new sections (which form the basis of much of this book) and following the enactment of the Violent Crime Reduction Act 2006, the Summary Review process was introduced into the Act via The Violent Crime Reduction Act 2006 (Commencement No. 3) Order 2007 on 1st October 2007, nearly two years after the Act came into force.

There are several distinctions between Standard Review applications under section 51 of the Act and Summary Review applications under section 53A.

---

4 Section 52(2) Licensing Act 2003

5 Section 52(11) Licensing Act 2003

Firstly, a Standard Review application can be initiated by any person.[6] This includes any responsible authority but also 'Other Persons' under the Act. In terms of the latter, this is frequently disgruntled local residents who are unhappy about the way the local pub is operated, usually for reasons of nuisance. There is a power for Licencing Authority to reject a Standard Review application made by an 'Other Person' on the grounds of it being frivolous, vexatious or repetitious but this power is rarely exercised.[7] In contrast, a Summary Review can only be initiated by the Chief Officer of Police.[8]

Secondly, a Standard Review application can be brought on any ground, and should be accepted as valid by the Licensing Authority as long as it is relevant to at least one of the Licensing Objectives. There is no requirement under the Act for the Standard Review of a Premises Licence to be sought on any prescribed ground save for the overarching principle of its relevance to the promotion of the Licensing Objectives. A Summary Review can only be brought if it contains grounds associated with the prevention of crime and disorder, and where that crime and/or disorder is serious.[9] There is nothing in the Act precluding the Chief Officer of Police including any other ground(s) in their Summary Review application, relevant to one of the other Licensing Objectives, but it must contain core grounds based on serious crime being associated with the premises to which the application is subject.

---

6 Section 51(1) Licensing Act 2003

7 Section 51(4) Licensing Act 2003

8 Section 53A(1) Licensing Act 2003

9 Section 53A(1)(b) Licensing Act 2003

Thirdly, is the Representation Period. For a Standard Review application this is 28 days beginning on the day after the application is received by the Licencing Authority.[10] For Summary Reviews this is 10 working days.

Fourthly, is the hearing itself which with a Standard Review is required to be held 20 working days after the end of the Representation Period (which is, give or take, one month) whereas for Summary Reviews this is within 28 days after the day the Licensing Authority receives that Summary Review application.[11] The overall process in a Summary Review is around half the duration of a Standard Review.

Fifthly, there is no mechanism under a Standard Review for any parts of the determination to take effect immediately. Under section 52(11) of the Act the decision does not take effect for 21 days from when it is delivered in writing, and if the decision is appealed against within those 21 days, until that appeal is disposed of. This difference between each power is perhaps the most impactful distinction upon licensed premises in particular, and was clearly the most important contrast to the legislators and the principal driver behind the amendments to the Act.

The Standard Review process is more widely accessible to applicants, less fast-paced and intense, and less immediately impactful on the licence holder and their business than the subject of this book, Summary Reviews.

---

[10] Regulation 22(1)(b) The Licensing Act 2003 (Premises Licences and Club Premises Certificates) Regulation 2005

[11] Section 53A(2)(b) Licensing Act 2003

CHAPTER TWO

THE SUMMARY REVIEW APPLICATION

The Summary Review process does not start in a police station or office of a police service, but in or near to a licensed premises. In the first instance it is not usually the Police Licensing Section within the relevant police service who are first aware of the incident that gives rise to the Summary Review application, which usually (although certainly not always) occurs on a weekend when the Police Licensing Sections are not routinely working (although compliance visits to premises most commonly take place on weekend evenings).

In the first instance it is usually a 999 call and frontline officers on duty at the time where the process of a Summary Review starts from a police perspective. The facts of the incident, if it has occurred on a weekend, often don't make their way to the relevant section in the police service until a Monday morning unless the incident has made the news over the weekend or is so serious that a senior officer unilaterally intervenes, which is unusual.

Assuming the incident involves an occurrence of serious violence then the necessity of the immediate and prompt investigation of the crime will mean that the premises will often be required to close in any event by officers at the scene as forensic protocols and procedures take place, and in fact a failure to close promptly in such circumstances (including before the police became involved) will often be used against a licensed premises in a subsequent Summary Review.

Upon the Police Licensing Section becoming aware they will be required to evaluate the incident to establish whether a Summary Review is necessary and to some extent, appropriate. This is where section 53A of the Act comes into play:

> ***53A Summary reviews on application of senior police officer***
>
> *(1) The chief officer of police of a police force for a police area may apply under this section to the relevant licensing authority for a review of the premises licence for any premises wholly or partly in that area if—*
>
> *(a) the premises are licensed premises in relation to the sale of alcohol by retail; and*
>
> *(b) a senior member of that force has given a certificate that it is his opinion that the premises are associated with serious crime or serious disorder or both;*
>
> *and that certificate must accompany the application.*

Senior member and serious crime are defined later in the section:

- *"senior member", in relation to a police force, means a police officer who is a member of that force and of or above the rank of superintendent; and*
- *"serious crime" has the same meaning as in the Regulation of Investigatory Powers Act 2000 (c. 23) (see section 81(2) and (3) of that Act).*

The first thing for the Police Licensing Section to establish is whether there is a Premises Licence at the venue where this incident took place and that the sale of alcohol is authorised on it.[12] This may seem like a straightforward matter but there are a significant number of premises that

12 Section 53A(1)(a) Licensing Act 2003

are licensed under the Act that do not authorise the sale of alcohol. These are most typically late night refreshment venues that only authorise the supply of hot food and beverage in any hours between 23:00 and 05:00;[13] this will incorporate (for example) any McDonald's open past 23:00 but also includes thousands of kebab, fried chicken, pizza and desert venues, including those that deliver hot food after 23:00. These venues were subject to stricter regulation than hitherto when the Act was brought into force in 2005, precisely because many of them were hot spots for violence in the early hours of the morning, most especially as weekends and the legislators wanted to bring them into a more focussed regulatory regime. Summary Reviews are not available for such venues and other statutory powers such as closure orders need to be considered by the relevant authorities there.

Perhaps surprisingly many Police Licensing Sections do not routinely hold copies of all the Premises Licences within their areas. Some local authorities (especially many in London) have an online register of the Premises Licences they issue, but the statutory requirement to keep a licensing register does not extend to the proviso that it is published online,[14] and so in some instances the only way the Licensing Police Service can establish whether the particular Premises Licence authorises the sale of alcohol with any certainty is by them contacting the relevant Licensing Authority and asking for a copy of the Premises Licence.

Alternatively, if the Police Licensing Section have already visited the premises in connection with the incident under investigation, then they may have already viewed the Premises Licence (assuming they don't have a copy themselves) as it is a requirement under the Act that the summary of the licence is displayed prominently in the premises,[15] and further that the full licence or a certified copy of it and a list of any relevant mandatory

---

13 Paragraph 1 Schedule 2 Licensing Act 2003

14 Section 8 Licensing Act 2003

15 Section 57(3) Licensing Act 2003

conditions applicable to the licence are kept at the premises in the custody or under the control of the licence holder[16] – although it is widely accepted these requirements (especially the display of the summary) are complied with by licence holders less frequently than any other under the Act! Obviously if that is the case then the police will no doubt be referring to this in their evidence in support of the Summary Review.

It would also be prudent for the Police Licensing Section to consider at this stage whether the licence was operational at the time of the incident. Whilst an answer in the negative isn't necessarily fatal to a Summary Review application, a serious disorder that breaks out on the pub car park at chucking out time is likely to be considered more closely associated with that particular licenced premises than a similar disorder that occurs a considerable time after the premises has closed and has locked up for the night. The facts of each case will inform the level of association with serious crime.

Once the authorisation of the sale of alcohol on the Premises Licence has been established then the Police Licensing Section must evaluate whether serious crime and/or disorder is associated with those particular premises. Whilst it is not ultimately the Police Licensing Section's call (as there will be no superintendent within that section, even in the Metropolitan Police Service) it would be wholly unrealistic and somewhat absurd if this wasn't the first evaluative stage of the process. In order to escalate the matter up the chain of command it must logically follow that those at the coal face must first have formed the view that a Summary Review is the appropriate course of action. In some instances, especially where a fatality is involved, this will be a very straightforward evaluation, however in others it may require a more considered and legalistic approach, which entails a statutory test, as is set out in Subsection 81(2) and (3) of the Regulation of Investigatory Powers Act 2000 ('RIPA'):

[16] Section 57(2) Licensing Act 2003

81(2) In this Act—

(a) references to crime are references to conduct which constitutes one or more criminal offences or is, or corresponds to, any conduct which, if it all took place in any one part of the United Kingdom would constitute one or more criminal offences; and

(b) references to serious crime are references to crime that satisfies the test in subsection (3)(a) or (b).

(3) Those tests are—

(a) that the offence or one of the offences that is or would be constituted by the conduct is an offence for which a person who has attained the age of twenty-one and has no previous convictions could reasonably be expected to be sentenced to imprisonment for a term of three years or more;

(b) that the conduct involves the use of violence, results in substantial financial gain or is conduct by a large number of persons in pursuit of a common purpose.

It should be carefully noted that Subsection 81(2)(b) crucially contains the word 'or' meaning that either of the tests in Subsection 81(3) can apply independently of each other; this affords senior officers huge discretion when evaluating whether serious crime has taken place in assortation with a licensed premises.

In terms of 3(a) it is unclear whether this is after a trial or when a guilty plea has been entered, which if done so at the first available opportunity would lead to a one third reduction in the sentence, and there is no case law on this point. This could be significant given the maximum sentence for both section 47 ABH and section 20 GBH (both under the Offences Against the Person Act 1861) is five years and so anyone entering a guilty plea at the first opportunity for either of those offences, where they are of previously good character, could reasonably expect a sentence of significantly less than three years. The attainment of 21 years is a clear nod to the fact that someone under that age, as a youth, could expect a less serious sentence than someone above that age. The 'reasonably expect' part (consciously, no doubt) provides a significant degree of latitude to police services when evaluating whether serious crime is engaged in relation to the particular premises in question.

In terms of 3(b) this is much less prescriptive and far more all-encompassing. The use of violence, as well as the foregoing GBH and ABH can also incorporate battery and common assault as well as possibly affray under the Public Order Act 1986, even in the absence of any identifiable disorder. Substantial financial gain is (doubtless intentionally) broadly worded and whilst most Summary Reviews relate to the use of violence or the presence of weapons, it is not uncommon (for example) for cannabis farms to be located in the non-trading areas of licensed premises or for convenience stores be used for fencing stolen goods; there have even been Summary Reviews that relate to stolen goods where the FBI and the National Crime Agency were both involved. All of the foregoing can provide valid grounds for a Summary Review application assuming the values involved and sophistication of the operation are sufficient, however a common sense and proportionate approach from police services is still necessary when applying Subsection 81(2) and (3) as a bit of pushing and shoving at the end of the night being considered serious crime is likely to invite ridicule.

There is no such definitive list of behaviours that constitute serious disorder, and the matter is one for judgement by the local police. The phrase should be given its plain, ordinary meaning, as is the case when applied under section 12 of the Public Order Act 1986, where this approach is also deployed when imposing conditions on public processions. Certainly, rioting and violent disorder are likely to amount to serious disorder, given the maximum sentences for each are 7 and 5 years respectively, and even though the maximum sentence for affray is three years imprisonment it often includes the use of violence and so may be captured. It is worth noting (although perhaps not crucial) that offences for rioting and violent disorder require 12 and 3 persons who are present together using or threatening unlawful violence for those particular offences to be made out.[17]

Judgement in relation to this part of the process is often defined by the particular police service it involves. Police Licensing Sections that are located in big cities such as London, Manchester and Birmingham have a wealth of experience in dealing with Summary Reviews, whereas those that are located in more rural parts of the country have much less experience, if any. In fact, there are a number of local authorities in England and Wales that have never been involved in a Summary Review despite the Act being in force for over two decades. The police services in the larger cities tend to have more of a feel for Summary Review applications simply as a consequence of trial and error, whereas the police services in the rural shires can sometimes have a tendency to bring a Summary Review when it isn't warranted, and on other occasions fail to when it was both necessary and appropriate to do so; however, as will be set out below, even if a Summary Review application is misconceived, the mechanism to stop that train once it is on the track is virtually non-existent.

Once the Police Licensing Section has arrived at the conclusion that the relevant behaviour amounts to serious crime and/or serious disorder then the next part of the evaluation process is whether serious crime and/or disorder is associated with the particular licensed premises. In many instances this will be straightforward: if there has been a shooting inside a nightclub then it is difficult to see how serious crime is not associated with those premises, but what about instances where an incident occurs outside the licensable area or even outside the building within which the licensable area is situated?

[17] Sections 1 & 2 Public Order Act 1986

The case of Lalli provides some specific guidance on this at paragraphs 46 to 48:

> *46. For one thing to be "associated with" another requires a relationship to exist between them, but the type of relationship that may be relevant will depend on what those things are and the context in which that phrase appears. In my judgment, for licensed premises to be associated with serious crime or serious disorder (in the context of section 53A of the 2003 Act), there must be a connection or link between them that could be relevant to the regulation of such premises.*
>
> *47. The mere fact serious crime or serious disorder occurs in, or close to, the licensed premises, therefore, does not necessarily mean in this context that such disorder or crime has any relevant connection or link with those premises. For example, disorder that has begun elsewhere and has nothing to do with premises, their management or customers might be continued in the road outside the licensed premises or might spill over into the premises' car park. The fact that the disorder has come to the licensed premises may have nothing to do with them. In such a case the disorder would have no connection or link with the licensed premises other than its accidental geographical propinquity to them. That could not constitute a relevant association between the licensed premises and the disorder for the purpose of regulating such premises.*
>
> *48. The nature of a relevant connection or link between the licensed premises and serious crime or serious disorder, however, may take various forms. It might involve a connection or link, for example, between the management of the premises or the activities of its customers or staff on the one hand and serious crime or serious disorder on the other. Given the inevitably wide and potentially unpredictable variety of circumstances in which serious crime or serious disorder may occur that may have some*

> *relevant connection or link to the licensed premises, Parliament has decided not to define or to limit the nature of the association with serious crime or serious disorder which the licensed premises must have. Parliament has decided instead to leave it to the opinion of a senior member of the local police force to determine whether the premises are associated with such matters.*

So as is often the case with purposefully worded legislation it is a matter of fact and degree based on the particular circumstances of each case, but once again it is the opinion of the senior officer that is central to this process and that opinion, unless it is one that no reasonable senior officer acting reasonably could arrive at, is essentially unimpeachable for the purposes of the Summary Review process.

Whilst the Guidance does ask the senior officer to consider the history of the premises in question there is no requirement for them to have any track record of problems in relation to crime and disorder, whether it be in relation to violence or other issues.

Again, Lalli addresses this point at paras 49 and 53 in particular:

> *49. Mr Phillips does not contend that there is any legal rule that the opinion of the senior member of the relevant police force giving the certificate cannot be based on a single incident. In my judgment that concession was rightly made. There is nothing in section 53A(1) that supports such a contention. Moreover, if correct, that contention would require what constitutes a single incident to be defined. A series of serious crimes might be committed which might or might not be classified as forming part of a single incident. In this case, for example, more than one serious crime may have taken place: one inside and one outside the pub. That might be classified as involving two incidents or merely as one continuing incident. But such a classification would not of itself cast any light on whether the premises were associated with serious crime.*

> *53. In my judgment, therefore, there is no legal requirement that that officer must be satisfied the licensed premises have been associated with any "pattern" of serious crime or serious disorder. There is no requirement that the premises are persistently associated, or that they have been repeatedly associated or associated more than once, with serious crime or serious disorder.*

Many Summary Reviews are made against licensed premises that have not previously been on the police radar. In such instances the licence holder is often incredulous, even bewildered at their involvement in the process, however the case law is clear that even in instances of premises with an exemplary track record, a Summary Review can be a wholly appropriate (and necessary) form of regulatory intervention.

At this stage the primary focus of the police will be around the protection of the public which is why in the overwhelming majority of Summary Review applications, a suspension of the Premises Licence is sought in the first instance

What constitutes the premises is a matter of ongoing debate in licensing circles and it is widely held to include (and only include) the area within the 'red line' that denotes the licensable area,[18] however there is case law from other, related legislation that suggests the definition may be wider than that. The case of Leeds City Council v Persons Unknown [2023] EWHC 1504 (Admin) deals with the issues of 'premises' for the purposes of the Antisocial Behaviour, Crime and Policing Act 2014 (the 2014 Act').

> *"In my judgment, "premises" for the purposes of Part 4 Chapter 3 [of the 2014 Act] calls for decision-makes to focus on whether there is somewhere objectively identifiable as being a distinctive property or distinctive part of a property. That means a property*

---

[18] Regulation 23 Licensing Act 2003 (Premises Licences and Club Premises Certificates) Regulations 2005

> *objectively identifiable, in the 'real world', 'on the ground'. I accept that the police, local authority or magistrates can take something which is a distinct part of an objectively identifiable property. So, it could be a floor within a block of flats or even a room in a bed and breakfast. I also accept that police, local authority or magistrates can take a building or structure. So, it could be the entire block of flats or a shopping centre. I also accept that premises can be identified so as to encompass adjoining or linked land or an adjoining or linked building or structure. Or premises can be identified which is land or a place which is open, or which is enclosed. But what, in my judgment, is always necessary is to identify somewhere, objectively identifiable 'on the ground' and 'in the real world', as a property. Beyond that, whether the facts and circumstances fit with the statutory language is a question of reasonable application for the primary decision-makers. Above all, "premises" are not an "area"; they are not a "locality"; they are not 'any line drawn on a map or plan'. Nor, in any event, do they include a "highway"."*

This point has yet to be determined in the context of the Act and it is worth identifying that the 2014 Act deals with all sorts of premises, many of which are not licensed and do not benefit from the subsistence of a line or other means to denote where the activities that are authorised are permitted to be carried on from. Lalli certainly provides no meaningful guidance on this particular point.

Once the Police Licensing Section have decided that the foregoing tests have been met then they will need to get an officer of the rank of superintendent or above to sign the requisite certificate.[19] An officer of lower rank (most commonly chief inspector) acting temporarily as a duty superintendent is sufficient. In fact, if this matter is so serious that it has come to the attention of the licensing section on a weekend, and the Certificate falls to be signed at that time, then it will often be a chief

---

[19] Section 53A(1)(b) Licensing Act 2003

inspector standing in as an acting superintendent who the request will be made of.

It is worth identifying at this stage from a police perspective that speed may be of the essence. Summary Reviews, as previously identified are also commonly known as expedited reviews and both terms suggest swift and decisive regulatory intervention. Whilst a few days here and there might not be crucial, any delay longer than a week, without any justifiable reason could be liable to frustrate the process, either in terms of the willingness of a senior officer to sign the Certificate or for the steps that are sought by the police in terms of an interim step being held to be necessary by the Licensing Subcommittee at the consequent hearing. Adequate reasons for a such a delay could be ongoing efforts to obtain evidence (such as an injured party being hospitalised and unable to make a statement for a period) or awaiting the evidence being available a viewable format

This stage of the Summary Review process will require the compilation of any evidence, and whilst not a strict requirement at this stage, a fully drafted review application being placed before the senior officer at the same time as the Certificate is an entirely sensible and appropriate step for the Police Licensing Section to complete at this early point in order that the senior officer can arrive at a fully informed opinion and know what will be placed before the Licensing Subcommittee in support of the Certificate that he is being asked to sign.

Once the senior officer has the relevant material before them, as previously stated, they are provided with a framework to evaluate the application by the Guidance:

> *12.7 In deciding whether to sign a certificate, the senior officer should consider the following (as applicable):*
>
> • *The track record of the licensed premises concerned and whether the police have previously had cause to give advice about serious criminal or disorderly conduct (or the likelihood of such*

conduct) attributable to activities taking place on the premises. It is not expected that this power will be used as a first response to a problem and summary reviews triggered by a single incident are likely to be the exception.

- *The nature of the likely crime and/or disorder – is the potential incident sufficiently serious to warrant using this power?*

- *Should an alternative power be deployed? Is the incident sufficiently serious to warrant use of the powers in Part 4, Chapter 3 of the Anti-social Behaviour, Crime and Policing Act 2014, or section 38 of and Schedule 6 to the Immigration Act 2016, to close the premises? Or could the police trigger a standard licence review to address the problem? Alternatively, could expedited [summary] reviews be used in conjunction with other powers (for example, modifying licence conditions following the use of a closure power)?*

- *What added value will use of the expedited process bring? How would any interim steps that the licensing authority might take effectively address the problem?*

12.8 It is recommended that these points are addressed in the chief officer's application to the licensing authority. In particular, it is important to explain why other powers or actions are not considered to be appropriate. It is up to the police to decide whether to include this information in the certificate or in section 4 of the application for summary review. The police will also have an opportunity later to make representations in relation to the full review. In appropriate circumstances the police might want to make representations to the licensing authority suggesting that they modify the conditions of the premises licence to require searches of customers for offensive weapons upon entry. Under the powers in sections 53A to 53D, this could be done on an interim basis pending a full hearing of

> *the issues within the prescribed 28-day timeframe or for an appropriate period determined by the licensing authority.*

Most Certificates tend to replicate much of the matters set out in the foregoing paragraphs 12.7 and 12.8 of the Guidance in the document itself; one such example is as follows:

> *I am a Superintendent in [ ] Police.*
>
> *I am giving this certificate because I am of the opinion that the summary review procedure is necessary to ensure the licensing objectives are promoted expeditiously. Given the seriousness of the trigger incident on [ ], in my opinion immediate steps are required that can best be achieved through the summary review procedures. Other steps available under the Licensing Act 2003, including a standard review application, cannot lead to the imposition of immediately effective steps to promote the licensing objectives and so these are inadequate. I view this application as a proportionate and necessary response to the serious incident at the venue.*
>
> *In coming to my opinion, I have had regard to the facts of the incident and current investigation, the terms of section 53A of the Licensing Act 2003 and Chapter 12 ("Summary Reviews") of the Guidance issued under section 182 of the Licensing Act 2003.*

In some police services the legal section and possibly their corporate communications team will be informed and consulted at this seminal stage, and it would be normal for lines of communication to be open with the Senior Investigating Officer in the criminal investigation to foreshadow any anticipated disclosure and evidential issues in the Summary Review process.

It is impossible to know with any certainty how diligently senior officers consider whether serious crime/and or disorder has been engaged. Given there is essentially nothing to gainsay that Certificate and the opinion that accompanies it, doubtless on occasions the Certificate is signed with only a cursory consideration of the evidence, but on other occasions doubtless the documents that are presented to the senior officer are subject to serious scrutiny and interrogation, possibly to the point that the Certificate isn't signed – although it is not possible to establish how frequently this happens. Either way it is essential that the best available evidence is submitted to the senior officer at part of this stage of the process, not least because it means the application will be oven ready to be submitted to the Licensing Authority upon signature of the Certificate by the senior officer.

Once the senior officer is of the opinion that the premises is associated with serious crime and/or serious disorder then the Summary Review application, made by, or on behalf of, the chief officer of police must be made in the form which is set out in Schedule 8A to the Licensing Act 2003 (Premises Licences and Club Premises Certificates) Regulations 2005 (SI 2005/42) and that the application must be accompanied by the Certificate,[20] the form of which is not prescribed in legislation but typically contains the matters set out above.

Lalli provides some Guidance as to the interaction and relationship between the Certificate and the Review Application at paragraphs 43 to 45:

> *43. When considering the proper construction of section 53A(1) of the 2003 Act, it is important in my judgment to distinguish two matters:*
>
> *(i) the certificate given by a senior member of the relevant police force and*

20 Section 53A(1) Licensing Act 2003

(ii) the decision by the chief officer of that police force to apply for a summary review of the premises licence.

44. The certificate, which the senior member of the relevant police force is required to give, is one stating that in his opinion the premises are associated with serious crime or serious disorder or both. That certificate does not have to state, nor does the section require that officer to have formed the view, that an application to the relevant licensing authority should be made under that section for a summary review of the premises licence. Whether such an application should be made involves the exercise of a discretion vested by that section instead in the chief officer of that police force. Whether that discretion should be exercised may depend, for example, on the nature of the association which the premises may have with serious crime or serious disorder; whether the chief officer of police considers that the licensing authority should be able to consider taking interim steps pending the determination of any review and his view of the need for, or desirability of, any review of the licence to be completed expeditiously. But the question whether to make such an application is different from whether the licensed premises are associated with serious crime or serious disorder or both.

45. The different functions vested by Parliament in a senior member and the chief officer of the relevant police force **respectively**, *however, are obfuscated in the non-statutory guidance issued by the Home Office. Somewhat confusingly the sample certificate provided in that guidance invites the senior member of the police force giving the certificate to state that he or she is giving it because he or she is of the opinion that other procedures under the 2003 Act are "inappropriate", rather than providing the reasons why he or she holds the opinion that the licensed premises are associated with serious crime or serious disorder. Similarly paragraph [2.4] of that guidance invites the senior member to consider a number of matters in deciding*

> *whether or not to sign a certificate that are directed at whether or not an application for a summary review should be made (which is a matter for the chief officer of the relevant police force). Paragraph [2.5] recommends that these points are also addressed in the chief officer's application for summary review, although the prescribed form for that only requires the chief officer to give details of the association of the premises with serious crime, serious disorder or both (the existence of which is a matter for the senior member of the force giving the certificate) rather than the reasons why, given any such association, the chief officer is making the application for summary review. But, in any event, there is no advice provided in the non-statutory guidance on what may constitute an association between licensed premises and serious crime or serious disorder. I have, therefore, derived no real assistance on that question from its contents.*

Once the Certificate is signed and the review application completed along with associated evidence at that stage then they are ready to accompany each other on their way to the Licensing Authority within which the premises in question are situated.

CHAPTER THREE

THE LICENSING AUTHORITY'S ROLE UPON RECEIPT OF THE SUMMARY REVIEW APPLICATION

Once the Summary Review application and Certificate have been completed, the next stage in the process is that they are both served upon the Licensing Authority. What the Licensing Authority are required to do at this stage is set out in a prescribed form in Subsections 53A(2) and (3):

> *(2) On receipt of such an application, the relevant licensing authority must—*
>
> *(a) within 48 hours of the time of its receipt, consider under section 53B whether it is necessary to take interim steps pending the determination of a review of the premises licence; and*
>
> *(b) within 28 days after the day of its receipt, review that licence in accordance with section 53C and reach a determination on that review.*
>
> *(3) The Secretary of State must by regulations—*
>
> *(a) require a relevant licensing authority to whom an application for a review under this section has been made to give notice of the review to the holder of the premises licence and to every responsible authority;*
>
> *(b) prescribe the period after the making of the application within which the notice under paragraph (a) must be given;*

(c) require a relevant licensing authority to advertise the review, inviting representations about it to be made to the authority by the responsible authorities and other persons;

(d) prescribe the period after the making of the application within which the advertisement must be published;

(e) prescribe the period after the publication of the advertisement during which representations may be made by the holder of the premises licence, any responsible authority or any other person; and

(f) require a notice or advertisement under paragraph (a) or (c) to specify the period prescribed under paragraph (e).

The Licensing Authority referred to in subsection 53A(2)(a) is the council's Licensing Subcommittee and the interim steps available will be referred to later in this chapter. In computing the period of 48 hours mentioned in subsection (2)(a) time that is not on a working day is to be disregarded,[21] so whether the application is served on the Licensing Authority on a weekend or a bank holiday will make no difference to the timescale imposed upon them to determine the interim step or steps.

The full review referred to in subsection 53A(2)(b) will be dealt with later in this book.

The regulations referred to under subsection 53A(3) are the Licensing Act 2003 (Premises Licences and Club Premises Certificates) Regulations 2005 which govern procedures for applications under the Act.

At this stage it is important to identify that the Licensing Authority should not be questioning the opinion of the Senior Officer and whether

---

[21] Section 53A(5) Licensing Act 2003

the conduct alleged to be associated with the particular premises constitutes serious crime. Lalli is unequivocally clear on this point:

> *62. In my judgment the licensing authority is obliged to conduct the summary review even if it considers that the information available to the officer when he gave the certificate did not establish that the premises were associated with serious crime or serious disorder. Moreover, even if the senior officer of police or the chief officer of police subsequently change their opinions about the association of the licensed premises with serious crime or serious disorder or about the desirability of holding a summary review, the licensing authority remains under a statutory duty to determine that review within 28 days of the receipt of the application. When doing so, as explained above, the authority may consider representations that do not relate to the crime prevention objective (as well, of course as those which do) and, as section 53C(2)(b) of the 2003 Act states, the authority must then take any steps as it considers appropriate for the promotion of the licensing objectives, not merely the crime prevention objective.*

On this point, Lalli goes on to state:

> *70. In my judgment Parliament intended that the licensing authority should be entitled to treat an application for a summary review made by the chief officer of police as valid if it is accompanied by a certificate that apparently meets the requirements of section 53A(1) and has not been quashed.*
>
> *71. It is not obliged to consider whether or not it is liable to be quashed*

On this point Lalli also states at paragraph 65:

> *65. This contention sits very uneasily with the acceptance in the Claimant's grounds which Mr Phillips settled and in his own*

> *skeleton argument that, in the light of the decision in R (Byrne) v Commissioner of Police of the Metropolis [2010] EWHC 3656 (Admin), challenges to validity of the certificate may only be made by way of a claim for judicial review.*

Given the Licensing Authority will be the first recipients of the Certificate the likelihood of it having been quashed at that stage are nil and on that basis their clear statutory duty at this point is to carry out the administrative requirements imposed upon them by section 53A of the Act.

The first step for the Licensing Authority will usually be one of the two requirements under Subsection 53A(3)(a), namely to serve all the responsible authorities with the Summary Review application upon receipt because this can be done from the office. The other step contained under that subsection, namely to notify the licence holder, is not required to take place the same day, and so that will usually follow from the notification of the responsible authorities, the following day.

This part of the process is covered in the Guidance:

> *12.10 Within 48 hours of receipt of the chief officer's application, the licensing authority must give the premises licence holder and responsible authorities a notice of the review and should include a copy of the application for review and a copy of the certificate, and must also consider whether it is necessary to take interim steps (place temporary conditions on the licence). When calculating the 48 hour period any non-working day can be disregarded.*

The Representation Period provided for under section 53A(3)(e) is 10 working days beginning on the day after the Summary Review application and accompanying Certificate are received by the Licensing Authority.

The requirement to notify the licence holder of the Summary Review application under subsection 53A(3)(a) can often be quite fraught. It will fall to a licensing enforcement officer to visit the premises to hand deliver the Summary Review application and Certificate at the same time the application is advertised at the premises. This is frequently the first time that the licence holder will have any notion of the tsunami that is about to hit their business. They will usually be aware of the incident that gave rise to the Summary Review application in the first place (although not always) but it is unusual (although not unheard of) for there to have been any indication to them from the police service that their Premises Licence will be (or is likely to be) subject to a Summary Review application by that police service. This is a function of the expedited nature of the proceedings and often with consideration for the sensitivity to an ongoing criminal investigation. This can often be a bewildering experience for licence holders who have gone from opening their venue on a weekend night to having their entire business seemingly under threat from the relevant authorities in a matter of days. This is the most common stage in the process for the licence holder to seek legal advice.

It is also the stage in the proceedings that many licence holders can feel overwhelmed, a feeling that doesn't necessarily subside as the process takes its course. Their business precipitously comes under existential threat from the apparatus of the state, often because of some unforeseeable and random interaction between a couple of patrons the weekend before and many struggle to process that without being consumed by emotion, including anger. Often, and especially at this stage, the job of someone representing the licence holder is as much about taking them through the process as it is about liaising with other parties to the Summary Review.

This would also be the appropriate time for the licence holder, if they have an appropriate insurance policy in place which provides cover for loss of their Premises Licence, for them to contact their insurer or broker and notify them.

This visit to the premises by the licensing officer will also involve the advertising of the application at the premises.[22] This notice is required to be printed on light blue paper of at least A4 size printed legibly in black with a font size of at least 16, and to be displayed on or near the site of the premises to which the application relates where it can conveniently be read from the exterior of the premises by the public[23] – and in the case of a premises covering an area of more than 50 metres square, one further notice in the same form and subject to the same requirements shall be displayed every 50 metres along the external perimeter of the premises abutting any highway.[24]

The council is also required to display the notice at the offices, or the main offices, of the Licensing Authority in a central and conspicuous place; and in a case where the relevant Licensing Authority maintains a website for the purpose of advertisement of applications given to it, by publication of a notice on that website, a requirement which applies to pretty much all Licensing Authorities.

All the above notices must be displayed for a minimum period of seven consecutive days starting on the day after the day on which the relevant licensing authority received the application under section 53A, and the notice would normally include the following:

i. The fact that the application has been made by the police and the date it was received by the licensing authority;

ii. the name and address of the premises, or if there is no postal address for the premises a description of those premises

---

[22] Regulation 36A Licensing Act 2003 (Premises Licences and Club Premises Certificates) Regulations 2005

[23] Regulation 38(1)(a) Licensing Act 2003 (Premises Licences and Club Premises Certificates) Regulations 2005

[24] Regulation 36(1)(a)(ii) Licensing Act 2003 (Premises Licences and Club Premises Certificates) Regulations 2005

sufficient to enable the location and extent of the premises or club premises to be identified;

iii. the postal address and, where applicable, the worldwide web address where the register of the relevant licensing authority is kept and where and when the record of the application may be inspected;

iv. the date by which a responsible authority or any other person may make representations to the relevant licensing authority;

v. that representations shall be made in writing, and the postal and email address to where those representations should be made;

vi. that it is an offence knowingly or recklessly to make a false statement in connection with an application and the maximum fine for which a person is liable on summary conviction for the offence, which is unlimited.

Any defect in the notice is highly unlikely to invalidate or even frustrate the Summary Review application, as long as it is 'substantially compliant' and does not prejudice any party (*R (D&D Bar Services Ltd) -v- Romford Magistrates Court and the London Borough of Redbridge* [2014] EWHC 213 Admin) commonly known as the Funky Mojoe case) and it is even more unlikely that a higher court is going to hold that even where a notice isn't substantially compliant, that it will frustrate the process, given the public interest in such reviews as extensively set out in Lalli:

> *42...... The general context in which each appears is that of a scheme to enable a premises licence that authorises the sale of alcohol to be reviewed swiftly in the public interest when it appears that those premises are associated with serious crime or serious disorder or both and to enable interim steps to be imposed and maintained pending the determination of that review with a view to promoting the licensing objectives.*

The advertising of the Summary Review application is provided for in the Guidance:

> *12.25 The licensing authority must:*
>
> • *advertise the review inviting representations from any persons for no less than seven consecutive days, by notice as described in regulation 38 of the Licensing Act 2003 (Premises Licences and Club Premises Certificates) Regulations 2005 (SI 2005/42) and, if applicable, on the licensing authority's website (see regulation 38(1)(b) of the above). The relevant notices should be published on the day after the day of receipt of the chief officer's application.*
>
> • *advertise that any representations which the premises licence holder, responsible authority or any other person want the licensing authority to consider at the review hearing, should be submitted to the licensing authority within 10 working days of the advertisement of the review appearing.*
>
> • *give formal notice of the hearing no later than five working days before the day or first day on which the hearing is to be held to the premises licence holder and to every responsible authority.*

At this early stage the licence holder (upon notification of the Summary Review application) and the police should seek to establish the provisional date of the final hearing with the Licensing Authority which may have already been identified at this point; certainly consideration should be given to the licence holder as part of this process, especially if they have already identified someone to represent them and their availability on a particular day may be an issue, but it needs to be borne in mind that there is no scope to move the review hearing date outside the 28 day statutory hearing window and some local authorities are considerably more flexible than others when it comes to listing hearings under the Act. However, the right of the licence holder to be represented by someone suitably experienced, given what is at stake for them, is something that a Licensing Authority should give considerable weight to when considering any requests around the date of the full review hearing.

Once the administrative requirements around notification by the Licensing Authority have been complied with then matters will move on the interim step part of the process.

CHAPTER FOUR

INTERIM STEPS PENDING REVIEW

Whilst this part of the process is ongoing the clock is already ticking. At the same time that the Licensing Authority are notifying responsible authorities, the licence holder and advertising the Summary Review application, the Council's Committee Services, in conjunction with the Licensing Authority, will be frantically trying to organise the first 'hearing'. This has been put in quotation marks because there is no requirement that it operates in accordance with what would normally constitute a hearing.

At this stage, the previous experience of the Licensing Authority will come into play. Big city local authorities by dint of previous experience will have a well-established protocol and a list of councillors who have previously proved willing to sit on a hearing at such short notice; smaller councils can find the novel experience significantly more challenging, but the statue is clear that whatever type of local authority, they are all required to make the determination on the interim step within 48 hours of receiving the Summary Review application.[25] It may well be in those less experienced councils that they will involve their legal section or even external independent counsel to advise about the process at this relatively early stage.

This part of the process can be assisted on both side by early (and pre-application submission) discussions between the police and the Licensing Authority, the latter of which can sometimes informally ask the police to delay the submission of the application for a short period (say 24 hours) in order that they can more readily comply with their statutory

[25] Section 53A(2)(a) Licensing Act 2003

obligations to determine the interim step within the prescribed time-limit. The police's main motivation when seeking a suspension of a premises licence is with the following weekend in mind, rather than the normally quieter days in the week. As part of those discussions the Licensing Authority may also make a request of the police about the specific timing of the submission of the Summary Review application (discrete from the day of its submission) as serving it towards the end of a working day, provides more flexibility for the recipient Licensing Authority than one that is served early in the morning.

This part of the process is governed by section 53B of the Act:

53B Interim steps pending review

> *(1) This section applies to the consideration by a relevant licensing authority on an application under section 53A whether it is necessary to take interim steps pending the determination of the review applied for.*

The test of necessity is distinct from the prevailing test across the rest of the Act's regime, including the subsequent steps in the Summary Review process, namely one of appropriateness,[26] although it is a distinction that is often difficult to distinguish. When something stops being necessary and becomes merely appropriate is not a straightforward matter to evaluate.

Subsection 53B(2) gives significant latitude to Licensing Authorities about the way this part of the process is determined:

---

26 Section 109 Police Reform and Social Responsibility Act 2011

> *(2) The consideration may take place without the holder of the premises licence having been given an opportunity to make representations to the relevant licensing authority.*

This subsection can be a controversial one and notwithstanding the clear flexibility it affords Licensing Authorities, most councils do invite the licence holder to a hearing, if feasible, where the necessity of the interim step is considered.

The force of Subsection 53B(2) is dealt with in some detail in the Guidance:

> *12.11 The licensing authority may want to consult the police about the steps that it thinks are necessary, pending the determination of the review, to address the immediate problems with the premises, in particular the likelihood of serious crime and/or serious disorder. The licensing authority may consider the interim steps without the holder of the premises licence having been given an opportunity to make representations. This does not, of course, mean that the licensing authority cannot afford such an opportunity if it thinks it appropriate and feasible to do so in all the circumstances.*
>
> *12.12 The determination of interim steps is not a matter that may be delegated to an officer of the licensing authority. The relevant decisions are likely to be taken by a licensing sub-committee rather than the full committee. It should also be noted that there is no requirement for a formal hearing in order to take interim steps. This means that the relevant sub committee members can communicate by telephone or other remote means in order to reach a decision. A written record should always be produced as soon as possible after a decision is reached.*

Many, if not most Licensing Authorities will convene a hearing in the routine way for them. With some councils that will be in person and with others it will be remotely,[27] although some use the latter for the interim steps hearing when they normally operate via the former in order to comply with the statutory time limits and not require their members to travel to the town hall, or council offices at especially short notice.

Subsection 53B(3) contains the steps that the licensing authority must consider taking at this stage:

> *(a) the modification of the conditions of the premises licence;*
>
> *(b) the exclusion of the sale of alcohol by retail from the scope of the licence;*
>
> *(c) the removal of the designated premises supervisor from the licence;*
>
> *(d) the suspension of the licence.*
>
> *For the purposes of subsection (a) the conditions of a premises licence are modified if any of them is altered or omitted or any new condition is added.*

The Licensing Subcommittee are not compelled to take any of the above steps, and could take no action at all against the licence, although this would only occur in the most unusual of circumstances, especially if the licence holder was not able to make any representations upon the review application and the only documents and submissions they would have to consider was those emanating from the police, as applicant to the Summary Review.

Moreover, in the vast majority of instances at this stage in proceedings Subsections (a) (b) and (c) are otiose, at least in isolation with Subsection

[27] Regulation 21 Licensing Act 2003 (hearings) Regulations 2005 and affirmed in Walk Safe Security Services Ltd v London Borough of Lewisham [2024] EWHC 1787 (Admin)

(d). The police have requested a Summary Review of the Premises Licence because in the opinion of a senior officer of that police service those premises are associated with serious crime and they will want the licence summarily suspending at that stage pending further investigations in all but the most unusual of circumstances.

The simple reality with this part of the process is that in a senior officer's opinion those particular premises are associated with serious crime and/or serious disorder, and that the police will almost certainly be seeking a suspension of the licence, and it would be a brave Licensing Subcommittee that didn't follow that suggested path at that seminal stage, especially with the safeguards that are provided later in section 53B for the licence holder to subsequently and promptly make representations against that step.

There has been an increasing trend in recent years for Licensing Subcommittees to invoke both subsections (b) and (d) together and suspend the licence **and** remove the DPS as an interim step. This approach serves absolutely no practical purpose whatsoever. The DPS is the nominated individual who authorises the sale of alcohol through the premises licence, which is a legal impossibility on a licence that is subject to suspension. This is appears to be a path where Licensing Subcommittees wish to convey their performative disproval at what has taken place, but at this early stage it is often difficult to establish where (if anywhere) the blame lies for what has taken place and it can often paint the Licensing Subcommittee into a wholly avoidable corner when the suspension of the licence serves the same effect.

One thing that is worth noting at this stage is that the suspension of the licence does not mean that the premises is required to cease operating. Obviously in a bar or nightclub the cessation of licensable activities, most notably the sale of alcohol and the performance of regulated entertainment, render the business to be effectively inoperable, however with a food-led operation such as a restaurant the premises can still lawfully serve hot food and beverage until 23:00 and patrons can bring their own alcohol for consumption on the premises, however the licence holder should be alive to the potential reputational consequences of such a step especially at an early stage in proceedings. Moreover, it should also be noted that in certain instances where it was felt by the police that the premises was especially culpable or the behaviour was likely to continue as a consequence this approach of continuing to operate the business with a suspended licence, some police services will consider also issuing a Closure Notice under section 76 of the Crime, Policing and Antisocial Behaviour Act 2014 to extend the scope of the regulatory restrictions imposed upon the business by requiring it to close. As will be identified in the next paragraph, if made in conjunction with a Summary Review application, this approach should be avoided by police services if possible.

In terms of Closure Notices there is ongoing debate about their deployment in relation to licensed premises. Closure Notices can be issued by either the police or a local authority[28] and are the precursor for an application for a Closure Order at a Magistrates' Court some 48 hours later.[29] These orders can initially be for a period of up to three months,[30] but can be extended for a further three months upon further application to the court.[31] Where such an Order is made and there is a Premises Licence in situ then that automatically triggers a review of the licence under section 167 of the Act.[32] The main practical distinction between the two regimes is that a Closure Order has scope to close the entirety of the premises, rather than merely serve to suspend the Premises Licence, and may be more suitable to pursue in circumstances where criminal activity has been taking place outside the licensable area or not directly in connection with licensable activities, such as a cannabis farm in the attic; however, whilst these is no lawful power to prevent Police Licencing

28 Section 76(1) The Antisocial Behaviour Police and Crime Act 2014

29 Section 80(3) The Antisocial Behaviour Police and Crime Act 2014

30 Section 80(6) The Antisocial Behaviour Police and Crime Act 2014

31 Section 82 The Antisocial Behaviour Police and Crime Act 2014

32 Section 80(9) The Antisocial Behaviour Police and Crime Act 2014

Sections applying for both around the same time, extreme caution should be advised about so doing as the timescales are wholly different and there is no mechanism to join the two processes – and this would be likely to make things more complicated and costly than they need to be.

The effect of this Summary Review interim step decision is that takes effect immediately or as soon after that as that authority directs.[33] There is a general requirement under regulation 34 of the Hearings Regulations that any decision does not take effect until it is given in writing, however the wording of subsection 53B(5) would appear that the interim step decision takes effect whenever it is orally delivered by the Licensing Subcommittee:

> *(5) Where on its consideration of whether to take interim steps the relevant licensing authority does take one or more such steps—*
>
> *(a) its decision takes effect immediately or as soon after that as that authority directs; but*
>
> *(b) it must give immediate notice of its decision and of its reasons for making it to—*
>
> *(i) the holder of the premises licence; and*
>
> *(ii) the chief officer of police for the police area in which the premises are situated (or for each police area in which they are partly situated).*

The word 'but' in Subsection 53B(5)(a) clearly distinguishing two discrete events, with a separate requirement under Subsection 53B(5)(b) that the decision is immediately given in writing (as per Regulation 34 of the Hearings Regulations), along with the reasons for making it to the

---

33 Section 53B(5) Licensing Act 2003

holder of the premises licence; and the chief officer of police for the police area in which the premises are situated.

This part of the process is dealt with extensively by the Guidance:

> ***The licensing authority and interim steps pending the review***
>
> *12.14 If the licensing authority decides to take steps at the initial interim stage:*
>
> • *the decision takes effect immediately, or as soon after it as the licensing authority directs; but*
>
> • *the licensing authority must give immediate notice of its decision and its reasons for doing so to the holder of the premises licence and the chief officer of police who made the application. The 2003 Act does not specify that the immediate notice has to be in writing. However, in an individual case the licensing authority may consider that the need for immediate communication at least initially requires a non-written approach, such as a telephone call. This may happen when, for example, the authority decides that the decision should have immediate effect. In such a case, the decision and the reasons for it should be explained clearly and in full to the licence holder (or someone who may properly act for the licence holder), and the call followed up as soon as possible with a written version of the decision and the reasons (for example, by email or fax) which is identical to, or not significantly different from, the version given by telephone.*

Sometimes, given the speed at which matters have moved, it isn't possible to effectively notify the licence holder of the Summary Review application or any subsequent decision; this is especially the case with premises that have not previously been on the police's or the Licensing Authority's radar, in particular where they don't have any current contact details other than the address of the premises, and especially where the venue only opens on a weekend. In such instances all the Licensing Authority's officers can do is post and hand deliver the decision and be vigilant around the use of the premises in the days ahead. The intervention of the local press may assist in getting the message to the licence holder at this stage and certainly the blue notice outside the premises advertising the Summary Review application should also provide a strong clue!

There is provision in the Guidance for other steps other than a suspension under section 53B(3):

> *12.15 The licensing authority, in deciding when its decision on interim steps should take effect, should consider the practical implications of compliance in relation to the premises. For example to comply with a modification of the conditions of a licence that requires employment of door supervisors, those running the premises may need some time to recruit appropriately qualified and accredited staff.*
>
> *12.16 In addition, very careful consideration needs to be given to interim steps which would require significant cost or permanent or semi-permanent adjustments to premises which would be difficult to remove if the outcome of the subsequent full review was to withdraw or modify those steps. For example, making structural changes, installing additional CCTV or replacing all glassware with safer alternatives may be valid steps, but might be disproportionate if they are not likely to be deemed necessary following the full review (or any subsequent appeal). The focus for interim steps should be on the immediate measures that are necessary to prevent serious crime or serious disorder occurring.*

These parts of the Guidance are of little practical use at this stage of the process given the overwhelming frequency at which a suspension is imposed at this point, but may be applicable later in the process, especially if a representation is made against the interim step of suspension and the appropriateness of certain conditions is up for debate.

At this stage it may seem to an independent observer, and certainly does seem to many licence holders, that a Summary Review application is a draconian power, however the case of Lalli expressly refutes that:

> *41. In my judgment a summary review is not a "draconian" power.*
>
> *i) A summary review involves the determination of the civil rights of the licensee. But the fact that it must be completed more quickly than a non summary review, within 28 days of receipt of the application for it, does not mean that the procedure governing the review itself is unfair or that the provisions are incompatible with article 6 of the Convention for the Protection of Human Rights and Fundamental Freedoms. They plainly are not.*
>
> *ii) It is, of course, the case that, having received an application for a summary review, a licensing authority is required to consider, and it has the power to impose and maintain, "interim steps" pending the determination of that review and that no compensation is payable for any loss that anyone adversely affected by such interim steps may suffer in the event that less restrictive or no measures affecting that person are imposed when the summary review is determined (whether by the licensing authority itself or by a magistrates' court on appeal). However, the legislation provides both procedural and substantive safeguards.*
>
> *(a) The decision whether any "interim steps" should be imposed does not lie with the police: it is vested in the licensing authority for the area.*

(b) Although that authority may act urgently without first hearing from others, it must hold a prompt hearing into any representations made in respect of them.

(c) Moreover any "interim steps" may only be ordered by a relevant licensing authority when "necessary" with a view to promoting the licensing objectives and they may only be maintained if "appropriate" for those purposes. Thus "interim steps" may not be imposed as a penalty or sanction (whether "draconian" or otherwise) for anything that may *have occurred in connection with the licensed premises. They are measures to be imposed only for preventive purposes when required in the public interest.*

iii) Further, although the interim steps and the outcome of the review may involve an interference with the peaceful enjoyment of a licensee's possessions for the purpose of article 1 of the First Protocol to the Convention for the Protection of Human Rights and Fundamental Freedoms17, the provisions governing them are plainly not incompatible with the licensee's rights under that article: they enable a fair balance to be preserved, subject to appropriate safeguards (including judicial review), between the public interest in the proper regulation of licensed premises and the licensee's interests. Indeed, anyone (such as the Claimant in this case) granted a premises licence after October 1st 2007 (when the provisions for summary review came into effect) has only obtained such a licence under a regime providing for such a review, including provision for the imposition of "interim steps" pending its determination.

42. In my judgment, therefore, the relevant provisions are not penal, much less "draconian". They each fall to be construed so as to ascertain the intention of Parliament as expressed in the language it used, in the context in which the provision appears, having regard to the purpose for which it was enacted. The

> *general context in which each appears is that of a scheme to enable a premises licence that authorises the sale of alcohol to be reviewed swiftly in the public interest when it appears that those premises are associated with serious crime or serious disorder or both and to enable interim steps to be imposed and maintained pending the determination of that review with a view to promoting the licensing objectives.*

One thing that can mark this part of the process is an inevitable consequence of the expeditious nature of the process. At this stage the evidence is at a highly developing stage and the culpability of the premises (or otherwise) frequently not fully established, or established at all. Conclusions and inferences are often drawn which don't represent the full picture. For example, there have been instances where the Summary Review application contains allegations that the premises did not call 999 when an incident of violence occurred at their venue, which has been taken by the Police Licensing Section from viewing their own police service's call logs; and whilst that has been correct what wasn't clear at that stage was that the premises managed to contact the police by other means such as finding a police officer on the street near to the venue and notifying them directly knowing that would be a quicker way of alerting the authorities and reacting to the incident than calling 999 on a Saturday night.

All this serves to underline the prudence of more temperate language in the wording of the Summary Review application than is perhaps instinctive for Police Licensing Section to deploy at that stage. There is a tendency amongst police services to use robust, definitive and binary language in Summary Review application which is often unnecessary and can serve to somewhat paint them into a corner down the line. One such example is the use of the hackneyed expression of them having' no confidence in the licence holder' at a particular premises in the Summary Review application only for a Licensing Subcommittee to then be faced with a representation against the suspension a couple of weeks later that is unopposed by the police! There is no need to use such strident language, or to make any particular value judgements in a Summary Review application, in the first instance. The fact that the premises that has a licence that authorises the sale of alcohol and which is associated with serious crime is usually sufficient in the first instance to obtain a suspension without rushing to make unnecessary statements about the culpability of the licence holder at such an early stage when the full picture has not yet emerged. It wouldn't be a stretch to say at this stage that if their administrative obligations have been met by the police, and the Summary Review application and accompanying Certificate are cogently worded, and they are asking for a suspension, then if that isn't the outcome there is a strong argument that the Summary Review application should not have been made in the first place.

This inevitable inchoate evidential picture at this stage can also be dangerous for licence holders if they are invited to attend the hearing and they do so, especially if they are unrepresented. There is a natural tendency for people to want to defend themselves, in particular when they are being accused of something which they feel is neither fair nor correct, especially where their livelihood is at stake, but they need to be extremely cautious at this stage of proceedings as to what they say, given they are likely to be asked questions by the members and possibly the police about the matters they assert and the issue that gave rise to the Summary Review application in the first place. Licence holders should go into any such interim step hearing in the knowledge that the police are going to be asking for a suspension, they are almost certainly going to get it, and given that, they should be careful to avoid saying anything that is not entirely necessary at that stage other than to say they are shocked at the incident and intend to work closely with the police in the days ahead to get a clearer picture of what has happened. Many licence holders have lost their licence at the end of the process simply by turning up unrepresented at the initial interim steps stage and saying the wrong things when the best they were ever going to get out of the proceedings at that stage was the suspension of their licence in any event. Often it is better at his stage that the licence holder does not attend at all, especially if they are not represented.

The decision under section 53A(3) will need to be communicated to the licence holder in writing, even if it has already taken effect, and there is no right of appeal against that decision to the Magistrates' Court, but it can be liable to swift challenge as will be set out in the next chapter.

CHAPTER FIVE

CHALLENGE TO INTERIM STEP

This is the part of the process where the licence holder, for the first time, has an element of control over the proceedings, albeit limited by the circumstances in which they have found themselves. This is also the part of the process that addresses their ECHR Article 6 rights (right to a fair hearing) which are arguably not present up to this stage in the absence of them previously being able to make any representations in person against the suspension of their licence, at least in front of some councils.

Although the Act is silent on this point it must naturally (and can only logically) occur after the interim step has first been imposed, and although there is almost exclusively a certain inevitability about a suspension being imposed under section 53B(3) at that stage, it would be a brave licence holder that challenged that step beforehand!

However, there is certainly nothing preventing that licence holder making such a representation as soon as they are notified of the suspension (or any other step available to the Licensing Subcommittee under section 53B(3)) but caution should be exercised before embarking on this path, despite the overwhelming instinct most licence holders will have to try and get the suspension lifted as soon as possible.

Firstly, except in rare circumstances where the Summary Review application has been demonstrably misconceived in some way, then unless the licence holder has some positive, active steps they can demonstrate to the council's Licensing Subcommittee as part of their representation against the interim step that in some significant and tangible way distinguishes the operation from when the incident occurred, then it is unlikely that the representation will be successful, and the closer to the interim step first being imposed the challenge is made, the truer that statement will be. Such steps are usually in the form of changes to the operation of the business made enforceable under the Act via condition(s) to be imposed immediately on the Premises Licence in substitution for the suspension, or possibly a change in DPS.

What conditions are appropriate to be imposed as interim steps at this stage will depend very much on the circumstances of the Summary Review application itself and what conditions subsist on the licence already. If it involves a knife being used (or brandished) within a licensed premises then a condition or conditions around searches of patrons (and even DJs and staff) and metal detection might be viewed as appropriate. If someone has been seriously injured, then putting all the staff on a first aid course might be seen as appropriate, in conjunction with other relevant steps such as a condition around crime scene preservation. If the incident took place in the early hours of the morning then a reduction in the hours for licensable activities may be viewed as an appropriate step – however these steps will rarely be a panacea on their own, especially if the police are not onboard, and care should be taken about suggesting a step that the premises is stuck with beyond the end of the Representation Period when the licence has been subject to a full review – this especially applies to any reduction in hours suggested at this stage, as there will be a temptation for the Licensing Subcommittee to leave any such steps on there at the full review hearing. It is a judgement call for the licence holder as they will need to suggest such steps as will be seen as adequate, but care should be taken about tying the premises' hand going forward in a way that hampers the business or even makes it unviable. A restriction placed on a licence that is unworkable may ultimately ~~often~~ have the same effect on the holder of the licence as one that has been revoked.

It is highly advisable that any proposed steps at this stage have been discussed with the Police Licensing Section, as well as the Summary Review more widely. Dialogue at an early stage, wherever possible, is widely encouraged under the Act, and if nothing else these conversations will enable the licence holder to establish the police's position and likely disposition towards the premises in relation to the full review of the licence.

Although not in the part of the Guidance that deal directly with Summary Reviews, paragraph 11.20 of the Guidance presents an overarching principle when it comes to (*inter alia*) licence conditions at any stage of proceedings:

> *11.20 It is expected that licensing authorities should so far as possible seek to establish the cause or causes of the concerns that the representations identify. The remedial action taken should generally be directed at these causes and should always be no more than an appropriate and proportionate response to address the causes of concern that instigated the review.*

To that end reference is made here to what was stated in the last chapter about police not gilding the lily in the Summary Review application. It is perfectly proper at this stage and in those circumstances to point the Licensing Subcommittee to the injustice of the Summary Review application where key matters alleged in therein have been proven to be materially wrong, but because of the regime and the prevailing associated case law the Certificate had to be taken on its face that and the licence under review was suspended as a consequence. It's a perfect opportunity for a tribunal of fact to do justice, if they can be nudged towards that outcome.

It is further worth considering at this stage what the Guidance says about conditions at paragraph 1.16:

Licence conditions – general principles

> *1.16 Conditions on a premises licence or club premises certificate are important in setting the parameters within which premises*

can lawfully operate. The use of wording such as "must", "shall" and "will" is encouraged. Licence conditions:

- *must be appropriate for the promotion of the licensing objectives;*
- *must be precise and enforceable;*
- *must be unambiguous and clear in what they intend to achieve;*
- *should not duplicate other statutory requirements or other duties or responsibilities placed on the employer by other legislation;*
- *must be tailored to the individual type, location and characteristics of the premises and events concerned; Revised Guidance issued under section 182 of the Licensing Act 2003*
- *should not be standardised and may be unlawful when it cannot be demonstrated that they are appropriate for the promotion of the licensing objectives in an individual case;*
- *should not replicate offences set out in the 2003 Act or other legislation; • should be proportionate, justifiable and be capable of being met;*
- *cannot seek to manage the behaviour of customers once they are beyond the direct management of the licence holder and their staff, but may impact on the behaviour of customers in the immediate vicinity of the premises or as they enter or leave; and*

- *should be written in a prescriptive format.*

These principles will also apply when the police are suggesting conditions at any point in the Summary Review process that are inappropriate or simply not feasible from the licence holder's point of view.

Secondly, and as indicated in the first point, the disposition of the police towards this representation against the interim step is a huge factor. If the police are not supportive of the suspension being lifted then it is significantly less than likely that the Licensing Subcommittee are going to lift the suspension, especially if they have imposed that suspension only a few days earlier; the suspension was deemed necessary by them at that stage based on a Summary Review application and accompanying Certificate as a consequence of this particular licensed premises being associated with serious crime; this will often involve someone who has been seriously injured, or worse, and the Guidance at 9.12 is clear on the role of the police in the licensing process:

> *9.12 Each responsible authority will be an expert in their respective field, and in some cases it is likely that a particular responsible authority will be the licensing authority's main source of advice in relation to a particular licensing objective.* ***For example, the police have a key role in managing the night-time economy and should have good working relationships with those operating in their local area. The police should usually therefore be the licensing authority's main source of advice on matters relating to the promotion of the crime and disorder licensing objective****. However, any responsible authority under the 2003 Act may make representations with regard to any of the licensing objectives if they have evidence to support such representations. Licensing authorities must therefore consider all relevant representations from responsible authorities carefully, even where the reason for a particular responsible authority's interest or expertise in the promotion of a particular objective may not be immediately*

> *apparent. However, it remains incumbent on all responsible authorities to ensure that their representations can withstand the scrutiny to which they would be subject at a hearing.*
> *[**emphasis added**]*

It is also worth noting that the Police are the only responsible authority who can object to the transfer of a Premises Licence or a DPS variation, only in exceptional circumstances, and only on the ground of the prevention of crime and disorder Licensing Objective being undermined by those applications being granted,[34] so their involvement in the process of applications under the Act is more involved and far reaching than any other responsible authority.

Furthermore, a Licensing Subcommittee would expect the licence holder to positively engage with the police as part of this process in the spirit of 'partnership working' encouraged by the Guidance and inevitably by their own Statement of Licensing Policy. A representation against a suspension a few days after it was imposed, in the absence of agreement, or even consultation with the police, is going to be a tough ask for anyone to get over the line in the absence of some significant flaw in the Summary Review application itself.

It is also worth being mindful at this stage that the Police Licensing Section will almost certainly be subject to pressures that extend beyond their own function. In most instances, especially where a weapon has been used, there will almost certainly be a resource intensive criminal investigation ongoing which will take priority over the licensing process for lots of reasons and sometime restrict it. These limitations can include certain evidence not being available in the review process for reasons which include not wanting to prejudice that criminal investigation in any way. These limitations can frustrate Police Licensing Sections and licence holders alike throughout the Summary Review process.

---

[34] Section 42(6) Licensing Act 2003

Moreover, Summary Reviews attract a lot more attention from senior ranks in the police than Standard Reviews; after all they are instigated following the opinion of a senior officer that those particular premises are associated with serious crime and/or disorder and often involve the commission of a serious offence which extends beyond the scope and reach of the Act, in terms of wider investigation and prosecution. Anyone advising a licence holder in Summary Review proceedings should therefore be alive to the fact that the people they are directly dealing with in the police may very well be subject to pressures from above to act (or not act) in a certain way. This pressure may also be driven by the family of any victim, especially if there has been a fatality. All of these factors are likely to influence the police to some extent, especially in the most serious of instances. It is important that this is factored in when dealing with the police as a failure to do so will often end in strategic miscalculation.

The disposition of the police towards the form and timing of any effort by the licence holder to lift the suspension of their premises licence will often be shaped by the spotlight that has inevitably been cast upon the licensed premises in question, as well as the previous operation of the licence more generally, especially when an incident of violence is involved. One of the first things that will be looked at is how the premises dealt with the incident in question. Did the venue call 999? If so, were the police called as well as the ambulance service? How promptly were they called? How was any victim, especially one that was seriously injured, treated by the venue? Was first aid administered? Was there any cleaning up of any evidence by the venue, either inadvertently or on purpose? How honest were staff and management with the emergency services and police when they arrived at the premises? Was the CCTV working as it should be when officers arrived at the venue? Was footage made available to officers at the scene, and was this footage helpful in the investigation of any offence? Did the venue continue trading when it was inappropriate to do so?

All of these things are highly likely to be fed back to the Police Licensing Section, including via bodycam footage from officers at the scene, and any CCTV footage retrieved from the premises, and unless there are reasons to withhold that footage in terms of the investigation of any offence, it will often be played in any subsequent hearings, whether in public or private.

Further, the spotlight on the premises will be cast further than the venue's immediate response to the incident that gave rise to the Summary Review application, or the incident itself. It will also almost certainly lead to a review of how compliant the venue was on the night in question (as it usually is in the evening or early morning), in terms of the framework of the licence and the venue's good practice more generally. This can range from the venue operating beyond its authorised hours at the time of the incident in question (which is always a challenging position to recover from) to breaches of the conditions on the licence more widely. Of most relevance and impact will clearly be those conditions that are relevant to the review itself that have (or have not) been breached. This will include door registers not being filled in as required under a condition on the licence, or CCTV not working as it should be. If there are conditions requiring the search of all patrons on entry that appear to have been compromised, then in instances where a weapon has been used or even brandished inside the premises this will be viewed especially seriously.

The Police Licensing Section or the Licensing Authority discharging its enforcement function, or possibly both working together, are also likely to look at the level of compliance with conditions more widely on the licence and will identify any areas whether the business isn't compliant. Refusals registers and incident books that are retrieved that plainly haven't been filled in for some time (or at all) is one such example of this.

The Summary Review application is likely to also cast a light on the compliance of the business in matters that extend beyond the Act, and stray into other regulatory fields: whether the door staff are suitably qualified and authorised by the Security Industry Association, whether the staff at the premises are entitled to work in the UK and if matters of public safety are engaged by the physical premises itself, then the Fire

Service may also want to intervene and make a representation upon the Summary Review application.

It is often these factors, rather than the incident itself, that prove key to how imperilled a licence is following a Summary Review application. A licence holder that can stridently state that they did everything they reasonably could to avoid the incident (especially one that was unforeseeable) occurring, because they were fully compliant with the conditions on the licence, as well as all other relevant legal requirements, will be far better placed than one that is on the backfoot because the CCTV wasn't recording when someone was knifed in their premises.

A third consideration is the optics more widely. Summary Reviews attract a great deal more attention than Standard Reviews, and are often headline news in the local press, and can frequently make the national media, especially if there has been a fatality. Care should be given around the sensitivities involved, again with a view to the feelings of the family of anyone affected by the incident that gave rise to the Summary Review application in the first place. A licence holder should always be conscious of how any steps in an effort to return the premises to where it was before the Summary Review application, especially those efforts that could be viewed as hasty, would be viewed by the wider public, and especially those affected by the incident, bearing in mind in particular that the individuals who will be tasked with deciding whether to lift the suspension of the Premises Licence will be elected members who will be conscious of the views of people who elected them into their roles.

It is important therefore that any licence holder, when making representations against an interim step avoids making too much (if any) reference to the financial impact of the suspension (or any other step) when seeking to persuade the Licensing Subcommittee to substitute the step they imposed for another.

That said, it is absolutely correct to recognise, and make submissions (sensitively) on the point that the licence holder is often the forgotten victim in these proceedings. Sympathy is quite rightly extended to the victim of any attack and their friends and family, as well as any witnesses, but it is often not appreciated the profound impact such an incident can have on an operator that extends far beyond the mere financial. Some licence holder's relationship with their business never recovers from an incident where someone has suffered life changing injuries (or worse) in their venue. It must be extremely difficult, if not impossible for any licensed business owner to move on from someone being murdered in their bar or nightclub, businesses that often never recover from such a tragedy.

Every case will be fact specific of course, but the decision as to when (and if) to make the representation will be a matter of judgement for the licence holder and whoever is advising them, and it should always be remembered that a misconceived and hasty representation is likely to be contrary to the best medium and long term interests of the licence holder, and it is important that those advising them do so robustly and in their best interests when discussing this part of the process with their client and push back where appropriate against a client who is (understandably) desperate to get their business open again.

It always far better if agreement can be reached with the police about the lifting of the suspension of the licence and to that end early engagement is essential.

The process for the representation starts in practical terms with the licence holder notifying the council of their intention to make it. This is usually best delivered by an email to the licensing authority. The following template may be useful.

> *Dear Licensing*
>
> *I act for the licence holder for the above premises and I am hereby making representations on their behalf under section 53B(6) of the Licensing Act 2003 ('the Act') against the interim step of suspension imposed by [insert local authority]'s Licensing*

Subcommittee on [insert date] under section 53B(3)(d) of the Act.

Please could you therefore arrange to hold an associated hearing within 48 hours of this email.

I have copied [insert relevant police service] into this email.

Kind regards

The email address to send such a representation will be on the Blue Notice on display at the premises.

There is no requirement to do anymore than send this notification to the Licensing Authority at which point the burden then shifts to them (although it is a matter of good practice that the police are copied in to this email) however any licence holder needs to seriously consider prior to this stage if discussions are ongoing with the police and especially if they appear to be progressing in a positive direction, notifying the Licensing Authority earlier than the foregoing representation that one is likely to be incoming on a particular date. This will be well received, and that level of consideration and courtesy can get back to the members sitting on the Licensing Subcommittee, which can never harm the prospects of the representation being successful. Even if discussions are progressing in a positive direction, or are not taking place at all, then if it all possible such advance notification is always better to provide if that is feasible and won't be contrary to the licence holder's best interests for tactical reasons.

When this representation is made then Section 53B(6) kicks back into play:

53B(6) Subject to subsection (9A), If the holder of the premises licence makes, and does not withdraw, representations against any interim steps taken by the relevant licensing authority, the authority must, within 48 hours of the time of its receipt of the representations, hold a hearing to consider those representations.

Once the representation has been made then as well as listing the hearing, the licensing authority is also required under subsection 53B(7) to provide notice of it to the licence holder and the police.

Again, as previously identified in respect of section 53A, and the imposition of the interim step, the time in the day that this representation is given to the Licensing Authority will have a significant bearing on the listing of that hearing, especially if no advanced warning of the representation has been given. A representation is highly unlikely to be accommodated on the day it is given for logistical and practical reasons, and so a representation made at 8am is only likely to be heard the following day, which will be the only remaining day available, whereas a representation made at 2pm on a particular day is likely to provide a greater degree of flexibility to all parties at it can be listed anytime the following day (most likely the afternoon) or the morning after.

One of the advantages with early engagement by the licence holder with the Licensing Authority about a likely incoming interim step is the possibility that as part of that interaction a likely time and date will already have been shared by the Licensing Authority before the representation is submitted.

The word 'hold' in Subsection 52B(6) suggests that the hearing should commence prior to the expiry of the 48 hours rather than the hearing be concluded by that point, and the decision arrived at within the time scale – otherwise the words 'have held' would surely have been deployed.

Subsection 53B 9A of the Act was inserted on 31st January 2017 via the Policing and Crime Act 2017, after certain legal professionals were in the habit of making repeated representations against a suspension of the premises licence in relation to the same Summary Review founded essentially upon the same basis, presumably in the expectation that their persistence would eventually prevail. Subsection 53B 9A is worded as follows:

> *53B (9A) Where the relevant licensing authority has determined under subsection (8) whether to withdraw or modify the interim steps taken, the holder of the premises licence may only make further representations under subsection (6) if there has been a material change in circumstances since the authority made its determination.*

This subsection is principally aimed at where the Licensing Subcommittee has declined to withdraw or modify any interim step taken, and needs to read in conjunction with subsection 53B(6) and notably the caveat of a withdrawn representation, necessarily made before the hearing commenced, would mean that the 'single strike' would not be used up, although the optics of doing so at the very last minute, given the level of organisation involved in convening such a hearing, will not be ideal for the licence holder and should be avoided if at all possible.

The material change in circumstances, as with much of the management of the hearing process more generally under the Act, is a matter of discretion for the Licensing Authority exercising its administrative function under the Act and its associated regulations. Some Licensing Authorities will accept a different proposed DPS or a further condition being offered as a material change, whereas others will look for something more significant, such as a change in the police's position. The only remedy available against such a decision by the Licensing Authority is that of judicial review which is simply not going to provide any solution in the time frame required. It is important therefore, when making such a representation that the reason for the material change in circumstances is expressly set out, hopefully with agreement of the police.

This part of the process is dealt with extensively in the Guidance

> *12.17 The premises licence holder may make representations against the interim steps taken by the licensing authority. There*

> *is no time limit for the premises licence holder to make representations on the interim steps, although in practice this would at some point be superseded by the full review which would have to be completed within 28 days of the application being received by the licensing authority. On receipt of such representations, the licensing authority must (if the representations are not withdrawn) hold a hearing within 48 hours of their receipt. When calculating the 48 hour period, any non-working day can be disregarded. Where the licensing authority has already held a hearing to consider representations against the interim steps, the holder of the licence may only make further representations if there has been a material change in circumstances.*

What constitutes the 48-hour period is contained in subsection 53B(10)

> *(10) In computing the period of 48 hours mentioned in subsection (6) time that is not on a working day is to be disregarded.*

So, (for example) the hearing for a representation against the interim step of suspension that was made on a Friday at 2pm would need to commence before 2pm the following Tuesday assuming the Monday is not a Bank Holiday, in which case it would be before 2pm of the following Wednesday.

The relevant licensing authority must give advance notice of the hearing to:

> *53B (7)(a) the holder of the premises licence;*
>
> *(b) the chief officer of police for the police area in which the premises are situated (or for each police area in which they are partly situated).*

So, even if this representation against the interim step is made (and not withdrawn) after the end of the 10-working day period for representations in relation to the Summary Review of the licence, under Subsection 53B(7)(a) the only parties to the challenge to interim steps hearing will be the police and the licence holder, even if other responsible authorities (and 'Other Persons') have made representations in respect of the review application. This serves to narrow the issues in the hearing to determine the representation against interim steps.

When fixing the hearing the Licensing Authority needs to give as much notice as possible to the licence holder and this is provided for in the Guidance:

> *12.18 The licensing authority must give advance notice of the hearing to the premises licence holder and the chief officer of police. Given that these measures are designed to deal with serious crime and/or serious disorder on an interim basis only, the process is designed to avoid delay and, as such, significant portions of the Licensing Act 2003 (Hearings) Regulations 2005 (SI 2005/44) (which set out the usual processes governing the conduct of licensing authority hearings) do not apply in order to streamline the hearing process. One result of this is that the licensing authority cannot adjourn the hearing to a later date if the licence holder fails to attend at the scheduled time, as is the case under the normal review procedure. And as is the case with that procedure, the licence holder does not have to be present for the hearing to take place. In addition, there is no timescale for notifying the licence holder of the hearing under the modified process, providing the notification takes place before the hearing is held. However, it is imperative that the licence holder be given as much notice as is possible in the circumstances to afford the holder a maximum practicable opportunity to prepare for and attend the hearing. Licensing authorities should bear in mind that the usual principles of public law decision-making will*

apply to interim determinations, in a form that has regard to the statutory context of an expedited process.

The steps available to the Licensing Subcommittee at this hearing are the same as under subsection 53B(3) namely:

(a) the modification of the conditions of the premises licence;

(b) the exclusion of the sale of alcohol by retail from the scope of the licence;

(c) the removal of the designated premises supervisor from the licence;

(d) the suspension of the licence.

For the purposes of subsection (a) the conditions of a premises licence are modified if any of them is altered or omitted or any new condition is added.

This limitation of the extent of the parties involved and the matters under consideration at the hearing to consider the representation against interim steps is reinforced at subsection 53B(8) and (9):

(8) At the hearing, the relevant licensing authority must—

(a) consider whether the interim steps are appropriate for the promotion of the licensing objectives; and

(b) determine whether to withdraw or modify the steps taken.

(9) In considering those matters the relevant licensing authority must have regard to—

(a) the certificate that accompanied the application;

> *(b) any representations made by the chief officer of police for the police area in which the premises are situated (or for each police area in which they are partly situated); and*
>
> *(c) any representations made by the holder of the premises licence.*

There is no right of appeal to a Magistrates' Court against the Licensing Authority's decision at this stage and this will most likely be stated in any associated decision notice.

It is worth noting that the test at this stage in respect of the interim step shifts from one of necessity to one of appropriateness.[35] In these circumstances this doesn't necessarily provide any particular advantage to the licence holder. If the decision to impose a suspension was deemed to be necessary, then this will weigh on the minds of the Licensing Subcommittee about what is appropriate following that.

It is also worth noting that the representation against interim step hearing (and the hearing that imposed the step in the first place) may be heard partially or fully in private. There is a presumption that hearings under the Act are to be held in public, and in fact most councils broadcast licensing hearings either on their own channel or externally such as through YouTube (and sometime both) but there is legal power to hold the hearing in private in certain circumstances.

This presumption of the hearing being open is contained in section 100A(1) of the Local Govermment Act 1972 ('the 1972 Act'):

[35] Section 53B(8) Licensing Act 2003

100A Admission to meetings of principal councils

> *(1) A meeting of a principal council shall be open to the public except to the extent that they are excluded (whether during the whole or part of the proceedings) under subsection (2) below or by resolution under subsection (4) below.*

Subsection 100A(4) and (5) provide as follows:

> *(4) A principal council may by resolution exclude the public from a meeting during an item of business whenever it is likely, in view of the nature of the business to be transacted or the nature of the proceedings, that if members of the public were present during that item there would be disclosure to them of exempt information, as defined in section 100I below.*
>
> *(5) A resolution under subsection (4) above shall—*
>
> *(a) identify the proceedings, or the part of the proceedings, to which it applies, and*
>
> *(b) state the description, in terms of Schedule 12A to this Act, of the exempt information giving rise to the exclusion of the public,*
>
> *and where such a resolution is passed this section does not require the meeting to be open to the public during proceedings to which the resolution applies*

Schedule 12A of the 1972 Act provides as follows:

> *1. Information relating to any individual.*
>
> *2. Information which is likely to reveal the identity of an individual.*

3. Information relating to the financial or business affairs of any particular person (including the authority holding that information).

4. Information relating to any consultation or negotiations, or contemplated consultations or negotiations, in connection with any labour relations matter arising between the authority or a Minister of the Crown and employees of, or office holders under, the authority.

5. Information in respect of which a claim to legal professional privilege could be maintained in legal proceedings.

6. Information which reveals that the authority proposes – (a) to give under any enactment a notice under or by virtue of which requirements are imposed on a person; or (b) to make an order or direction under any enactment.

7. Information relating to any action taken or to be taken in connection with the prevention, investigation or prosecution of crime.

Paragraphs 1, 2, 5 and 7 in particular can apply to a Summary Review hearing.

This power to conduct the hearing in private is further bolstered and expanded upon in regulation 14 of the Hearings Regulations:

Hearing to be public

14.(1) Subject to paragraph (2), the hearing shall take place in public.

(2) The licensing authority may exclude the public from all or part of a hearing where it considers that the public interest in so

> *doing outweighs the public interest in the hearing, or that part of the hearing, taking place in public.*
>
> *(3) For the purposes of paragraph (2), a party and any person assisting or representing a party may be treated as a member of the public.*

This regulation allows for the exclusion of any party from the hearing, including, in theory, the licence holder and their legal representative!

The licence holder should be asked their views by the legal advisor to the Licensing Subcommittee at the hearing about such an application from the police. Unless there is a compelling reason not to, this application should not be objected to by the licence holder. Firstly because it is unlikely that the public ventilation of the particulars that gave rise the Summary Review are going to enhance the reputation of the venue, and secondly to support such an application may also give the impression (impliedly or expressly) of support for the investigation of the crime – but also because it is inconceivable that such a request will not be acceded to by the Licensing Subcommittee, acting on legal advice, at least in part where the police have suggested that to conduct the hearing in public may prejudice the ongoing investigation into a serious crime. Choosing your battles is a key part of any licence holder's approach to Summary Review proceedings and making submissions that the hearing be heard in public when the police have applied otherwise as described above is not a hill that a licence holder should be dying on.

The licence holder should always have the full review hearing in mind when they are considering the representations against interim step. On the one hand, if the suspension is substituted for another step, such as a further conditions then subject to there being no incidents in the period between the suspension being lifted and the full review hearing, the issue of the ongoing suspension of the licence following the final hearing has been comprehensively addressed by the licence holder; this makes the final hearing far less replete with jeopardy – however licence holders should also be mindful about the possible consequences of offering an interim step that they cannot live with at the end of the process as it is quite possible (although not a given) that step will be maintained by the Licensing Subcommittee at the end of the process, which could only be overturned on appeal. This is especially the case with any reduction in hours.

Any decision in relation to a representation against the interim step effectively takes place immediately upon the oral decision being given, although most Licensing Authorities are assiduous about producing the written decision promptly thereafter or even at the same time.

CHAPTER SIX

REPRESENTATION PERIOD

While the period for a licence holder making representations against the interim step of suspension is ongoing, so is the Representation Period in respect of the Summary Review application itself.

This part of the process can (but does not always) bring other responsible authorities into the process, principally for one of two reasons. Firstly, is if the circumstances of the Summary Review are especially serious and touch upon that responsible authority's particular function, even in a relatively abstract way. Public health are probably the most common responsible authority to make representations upon Summary Review applications, but if the incident involves the use of a knife then trading standards may make a representation, as may child protection if the incident involved an individual under the age of 18, especially if they are a victim. Secondly it may provide a springboard for that responsible authority to raise an issue with another, subsisting aspect of the operation of the business that they were previously aware of. Most commonly this would be environmental health in relation to any noise nuisance issues at (or from) the premises, and the Licensing Authority especially if the police investigation has thrown up breaches of conditions on the licence, even if those breaches aren't directly linked to the matters that gave direct rise to the Summary Review application, although it should be remembered in respect of the example of the environmental health scenario that it would appear that the concerns they previously had weren't sufficiently serious for them to have made a Standard Review application in advance of the police's Summary Review application.

The Representation Period is a relatively brief one and because their heads are (understandably) elsewhere, licence holders often miss the fact that representations in support of the premises are entirely permissible, and can be especially helpful if they come from people who have lived in the vicinity for some time; petitions, whilst generally considered admissible by Licensing Authorities (although many have prescribed rules around their form in their Statement of Licensing Policy) are generally of limited probative value; however, bespoke representations talking of the responsible way the premises have been run over a period of time, and their place in the local community, can be hugely beneficial to a licensed premises in a Summary Review, although any such representation needs to be careful to make reference to, and frame the wording around the Licensing Objectives, and it should be further noted that Licensing Sub Committees have recently become increasingly alive to AI produced representations and these tend to be given less weight than ones that have demonstrably been considered and written by the representor themselves. It should be remembered that local residents who make representations in support of a premises are voters that the Licensing Subcommittee (who are politicians) will be conscious of being seen to be taking their views into account, especially if they are vocalised in person at the review hearing.

There is nothing wrong with the licence holder canvasing the views of those in the vicinity of the premises who may wish to make representations in support of the venue, but they should remind those individuals of the tight timescales involved, where their representation needs to go, and the fact that the email (assuming that is the method of delivery) ideally comes from them, not the via licence holder. From the licence holder's point of view this part of the process can be like herding cats. Any representations made after the end of the Representation Period will be rejected by the Licensing Authority as invalid, although there is nothing preventing the licence holder in those circumstances submitting them as supporting evidence for the full review hearing, although this will mean they will almost certainly be given less weight than if they had been submitted on time.

Making a representation that is deemed valid and relevant by the Licensing Authority will mean that 'Other Person' will have the right to make an oral submission in support of their representation at the final hearing, although some are understandably terrified at that prospect.

What constitutes a relevant representation is contained in section 53C (7) and (8)

> *(7) In this section "relevant representations" means representations which—*
>
> *(a) are relevant to one or more of the licensing objectives, and*
>
> *(b) meet the requirements of subsection (8).*
>
> *(8) The requirements are—*
>
> *(a) that the representations are made by the holder of the premises licence, a responsible authority or any other person within the period prescribed under subsection 53A(3)(e),*
>
> *(b) that they have not been withdrawn, and*
>
> *(c) if they are made by a person who is not a responsible authority, that they are not, in the opinion of the relevant licensing authority, frivolous or vexatious.*
>
> *(9) Where the relevant licensing authority determines that any representations are frivolous or vexatious, it must notify the person who made them of the reasons for that determination.*

The bar for a representation to be rejected as frivolous or vexations, or even not relevant is a very high one and most Licensing Authorities are highly reluctant to exclude members of the public from the licensing process and if this happens then certainly this should be challenged by the licence holder if those representations are in support of the premises, unless the representation is entirely irrelevant or incoherent.

The issue of representations' frivolity or vexatiousness is dealt with comprehensively in the Guidance:

> *9.5 It is for the licensing authority to determine whether a representation (other than a representation from a responsible authority) is frivolous or vexatious on the basis of what might ordinarily be considered to be vexatious or frivolous. A representation may be considered to be vexatious if it appears to be intended to cause aggravation or annoyance, whether to a competitor or other person, without reasonable cause or justification. Vexatious circumstances may arise because of disputes between rival businesses and local knowledge will therefore be invaluable in considering such matters. Licensing authorities can consider the main effect of the representation, and whether any inconvenience or expense caused by it could reasonably be considered to be proportionate.*
>
> *9.6 Frivolous representations would be essentially categorised by a lack of seriousness. Frivolous representations would concern issues which, at most, are minor and in relation to which no remedial steps would be warranted or proportionate*

It should be noted that different Licensing Authorities deploy different approaches when it comes to notifying the parties about any representations. Some drip feed them as they come in, and others release them *en masse* at the end of the Representation Period, however emailing enquiries to the Licensing Authority throughout the Representation Period should still elicit regular updates in councils that apply the latter approach.

CHAPTER SEVEN

THE FINAL HEARING

At the end of the Representation Period and no later than 28 days after the Summary Review application is received by the Licensing Authority is the requirement to hold a full review hearing, which inherently incorporates two decisions, which are both interlinked but wholly distinct from each other.

This hearing is dealt with in the Guidance:

> *12.22 The licensing authority must hold a full review of the premises licence and determine the review within 28 days after the day of receipt of the chief officer's application. There can be no adjournment of the hearing or delay in reaching a determination beyond the end of the 28 day period. This must take place even if the chief officer or other responsible authority and/or other person asks to withdraw their application or representation (as the case may be). At the review hearing, the licensing authority must consider what steps are appropriate for the promotion of the licensing objectives taking into account the application and any change in circumstances since any interim steps were imposed, consider any relevant representations, and review the interim steps already taken (if any).*

The report for this hearing is required under the Hearings Regulations to be published on the council's website five working days before the hearing.

In general terms, hearings under the Act are usually fantastic from a papers point of view, as they are required to be publicly published (although sometimes subject to redaction) and so are readily accessible in PDF form 24/7 at the appropriate time and *ad infinitum* thereafter.

At this stage the Representation Period is over and anyone who wants to make a representation in relation to the review application must have done so within the prescribed ten working days.

Unless the Summary Review application is highly publicised or the premises are associated with issues of nuisance, then notwithstanding the previous observations, it is not at all uncommon for there to be no representations at all upon the Summary Review application and in those circumstances the only parties at the final review hearing are the police and the licence holder. There are a couple of reasons for this. Firstly the issues in a Summary Review are often quite narrow, frequently being principally limited to the incident that gave rise to the Summary Review application in the first place; the other reason for this is that the Representation Period is shorter and so there is simply less opportunity for people to comment (positively or negatively) about the premises in question. The absence of any representations in support of the Summary Review is certainly a point for the licence holder to make at the full review hearing, but it is rarely going to be a killer point.

Assuming there are other representations at this stage, and there hasn't been dialogue with those representors by this point then it is usually advisable to do so. As previously indicated, it may be that public heath, in their capacity as a responsible authority will have made a representation, which are usually quite anodyne and broadly aimed at statistics in the local area more generally rather than the premises themselves – this feature is absolutely something that should be identified by the licence holder in the full hearing. Certainly, if a first aid course has been attended by the venue's staff prior to the review hearing, then this is something the licence holder may wish to raise with public health in an effort for that responsible authority to modify their approach to the Summary Review. This approach should be mirrored with other responsible authorities. Often the representation of public health will say it supports the Summary Review of the premises without actually requesting a particular outcome. Again, this is something, if maintained until the end of the hearing, should be identified by the licence holder in closing.

Other responsible authorities' representations are harder to predict and should be dealt with by the licence holder on an *ad hoc*, case-by-case basis.

Local residents (other than those in support of the premises) are a tricky one and the level of interaction with this cohort (if any) at this stage are a matter of judgement for the licence holder. They will usually fall into one of two categories. Firstly those that say they appalled by what happened at the premises and wish to express that publicly; secondly are those who have historical issues with the premises, often relation to public nuisance and antisocial behaviour, and look upon the Summary Review as a means to ventilate that. Sometimes the latter deploy the former approach to bolster their representation. Certainly, extreme caution should be exercised with engaging with the latter of those two groupings. Their issues are unlikely to be resolved by a meeting with the venue, as relations may have already moved beyond that point; that said, dialogue between parties is encouraged within the licensing regime and so suggesting a meeting to show willing, even if that offer is (as anticipated) declined, will at least show a willingness to engage with other parties as part of the process.

The Guidance provides for other procedural matters in relation to the final hearing:

> *12.26 A party shall give to the licensing authority a notice no later than two working days before the day or the first day on which the hearing is to be held stating –*
>
> • *whether he intends to attend or be represented at the hearing;*
>
> • *whether he considers a hearing to be unnecessary.*
>
> • *whether he would like permission for any other person (other than the person he intends to represent him at the hearing) to*

> *appear at the hearing and, if so, explain on which points that person will be able to contribute.*
>
> *12.27 The regulations relating to hearings are set out in the Licensing Act 2003 (Hearings) Regulations 2005 (S.I. 2005/44). They apply to final hearings under the section 53A(2)(b) in a similar way to hearings following closure orders under section 167 of the 2003 Act (it should be emphasised that the truncated version of the hearings regulations described in paragraph 12.18 above applies to interim hearings only). The issues they address include who can make representations and what those representations can be about. It is therefore possible for responsible authorities or any other persons to make representations in relation to any of the licensing objectives, not just crime and disorder. Similarly, where it is in the public interest, the regulations relating to the exclusion of individuals from hearings, or conducting the hearing in private, will apply.*

In advance of the hearing all parties should consider the submission of any evidence in support of their case. This part of the process is addressed in regulation 18 of the Hearings Regulations:

> *18 In considering any representations or notice made by a party the authority may take into account documentary or other information produced by a party in support of their application, representations or notice (as applicable) either before the hearing or, with the consent of all the other parties, at the hearing.*

The generally accepted convention in relation to that regulation is that 'before the hearing' means the day before at the latest, but it is important for all parties to take into account the volume of supporting material that they are likely to submit and consider the length of time that the members considering the review application in particular are likely to need to absorb the information contained therein in advance of the hearing. Annoying the people who will determine the future of the licensed business under review by dumping a huge amount of material at the last minute is unlikely to curry favour or assist those doing it.

Some Licensing Authorities have their own rules in relation to the service of supporting evidence, which will usually be contained in the Statement of Licensing Policy, however the legality of these rules is highly questionable as it seeks to override the express intent of the statute in regulation 18, and this is especially the case in relation to Summary Reviews given the tighter timescales involved and what is more immediately at stake to the licence holder – any Licensing Authority seeking to deviate from Regulation 18 in a Summary Review should be robustly challenged on this approach and be reminded about the inherent requirement that the Summary Review hearing operates in accordance with the laws of natural justice.

Around the same time of the notification, all parties should be sent the council's hearing rules, and these do vary from one local authority to another. The principal and most significant areas of difference tend to relate to the permissibility or otherwise of a party directly asking questions of other parties at the hearing, as well as time limits that are imposed on each party at some councils.

The requirement to review the premises licence subject to the Summary Review is contained in section 53A but reinforced in subsections 53C (1) and (2).

> ***53C Review of premises licence following review notice***
>
> *(1) This section applies to a review of a premises licence which a relevant licensing authority has to conduct on an application under section 53A.*
>
> *(2) The relevant licensing authority must—*
>
> *(a) hold a hearing to consider the application for the review and any relevant representations; and*

(b) take such steps mentioned in subsection (3) (if any) as it considers appropriate for the promotion of the licensing objectives;

Under section 53D there is also a requirement at the same hearing to determine the interim steps, which again was introduced as part of the Crime and Policing Act 2017.

53D Interim steps pending section 53C decision coming into effect

(1) At the hearing to consider an application for a review under section 53A, the relevant licensing authority must review any interim steps that have been taken by the relevant licensing authority under section 53B that have effect on the date of the hearing.

(2) In conducting the review under this section, the relevant licensing authority must—

(a) consider whether the interim steps are appropriate for the promotion of the licensing objectives;

(b) consider any relevant representations; and

(c) determine whether to withdraw or modify the interim steps taken.

The steps available in respect of 53C and 53D follow by now a familiar pattern:

53C (3) Those steps are—

(a) the modification of the conditions of the premises licence,

(b) the exclusion of a licensable activity from the scope of the licence,

(c) the removal of the designated premises supervisor from the licence,

(d) the suspension of the licence for a period not exceeding three months, or

(e) the revocation of the licence.

(4) For the purposes of subsection (3)(a) the conditions of a premises licence are modified if any of them is altered or omitted or any new condition is added.

There is also provision within Subsection 53C(6) that where the Licensing Authority takes a step within subsection (3)(a) or (b), it may provide that the modification or exclusion is to have effect only for a specified period, not exceeding three months, but this power is very rarely exercised.

The available steps contained within Section 53D in respect of the interim steps are as follows:

53D (3) (3) The power of the relevant licensing authority on a review under this section includes a power to take any of the following interim steps—

(a) the modification of the conditions of the premises licence;

(b) the exclusion of the sale of alcohol by retail from the scope of the licence;

(c) the removal of the designated premises supervisor from the licence;

(d) the suspension of the licence;

and for this purpose the conditions of the licence are modified if any of them is altered or omitted or any new condition is added.

Any interim steps taken under section 53B in relation to a Premises Licence cease to have effect when the decision made under section 53C comes into effect.[36]

It should be noted that for obvious reasons there is no scope to revoke a licence under section 53D.

Unless the decision is appealed then the hearing, held within 28 days of the Summary Review application and Certificate being received by the licensing authority, marks the end of the process, save for any subsequent appeal.

The hearing will be held in front of the council's Licensing Subcommittee, and it may be advisable to check as early on as feasible with Committee Services to see if any of the councillors that previously sat on any of the representation against interim steps hearings are also set to sit on, and thereby determine, the final hearing. There is nothing in the Act, associated Regulations or the Guidance preventing councillors from sitting on both hearings and nor will this be provided for the council's Statement of Licensing Policy, hearing rules or their constitution, but there may be circumstances where it is proper for a licence holder to raise concerns about councillors sitting twice in respect of the same Summary Review application. If the member in question sat on the first interim steps determination then this wouldn't normally provide adequate grounds to raise that, but if they had declined to substitute a suspension for some other step available under section 53B(3) in relation to a representation against the interim steps, especially if that representation was made relatively recently prior to the final

[36] Section 53D(5) Licensing Act 2003

hearing, and in particular if the submissions at the final hearing are going to be along the same lines as those that were advanced in the hearing for the representation against interim steps, then that councillor's ability to make a determination at the final hearing and **be seen to** be impartial may quite properly be called into question.

The legal test for such an evaluation is contained in Porter v McGill [2001] UKHL 67, namely: "would the fair-minded and informed observer, having considered the facts, conclude that there was a real possibility that the tribunal was biased?". This doesn't mean that the tribunal is necessarily (or definitively) biased but can also be founded upon the perception of possible, perceived bias, which can quite naturally be based on (*inter alia*) the decision-maker's past determinations, especially recent ones, or potential subconscious influences, which create a justifiable doubt about their fairness and ability to be impartial, or the perception of the same.

If the licence holder feels that a particular member is so tied to a previous decision that it would be difficult for that councillor to objectively form another view based on essentially the same facts (or be seen to) then this should be raised by them to the legal section at the council at the earliest opportunity. This certainly should not be raised at the hearing itself if this can be avoided, as given the statutory time limits involved there will be no realistic prospect of an adjournment and it may not be possible for a single member to recuse themselves at that stage because most council's constitutions provide a prescriptive number for a quorum at a hearing, usually three, and getting a substitute member in that time may prove to be impossible.

The hearing itself will be structured in many ways like a Standard Review hearing. There will usually be three members of the Licensing Subcommittee making the determination, who will be legally advised, sometimes by an in-house solicitor, although if the Summary Review is high profile it will often be independent counsel (and occasionally a solicitor in private practice) drafted in for the day for that purpose. The

Licensing Subcommittee will also be assisted by someone from Committee Services who will most likely take notes. There will also be a licensing officer or manager who will deal with the administrative part of the hearing including reading the relevant parts of the agenda report out at the beginning; they are also there to answer any questions about the history or structure of the Premises Licence but take no part in the decision making process and unlike the legal advisor and Committee Servies will be excluded when the Licensing Subcommittee deliberate.

Clearly the police will be there; it is their Summary Review application, after all. They may be legally represented, either by someone from their legal section, or again independent counsel. This will vary significantly from police service to police service – some will always instruct counsel for a Summary Review, others rarely and only in the most serious of such cases. Police officers and civilians within Police Licensing Sections, especially in big cities, are usually entirely capable and often extremely adept at conducting these hearings themselves, especially given the level of experience they will likely have of the process.

Present is also likely to be any of the other parties that have made representations (responsible authorities and/or 'Other Persons') who the licence holder may have been in dialogue with.

Lastly, because it is a public hearing then members of the public may be there as well as the local press although it may be that upon request from the police, as identified earlier, part or all of the hearing may be heard in private – this will usually depend at what stage any criminal investigation is at this point. Certainly, it is more likely at this stage that the hearing can be heard in public due to the effluxion of time and the evolution of any criminal investigation.

As it is their application the police would be expected to go first and at the end of their presentation (whether time limited or not) the members of the Licensing Subcommittee will have the opportunity to ask questions of them, and depending on the council's particular hearing rules, the other parties to the hearing may too. It is also possible, and is increasingly *de rigueur,* for the legal adviser to ask questions at the same time as the members or on an *ad hoc* basis as matters arise.

If representations have been made then the process will be repeated for those representors, although some local authorities encourage or even require that when there are a number of representations from local residents and businesses, especially where those representations are along the same lines, then one of their number is often invited to make representations on behalf of all of them, or that their time is limited overall, to the same as each other party to the hearing has individually.

In circumstances where asking questions of other parties to the hearing is permitted, extreme caution should be exercised by the licence holder in relation to 'Other Persons' who have made representations in support of the Summary Review. This is partly because such questioning provides an avoidable opportunity for those individuals to further ventilate their grievances, but also, especially where the licence holder is legally represented, questioning that descends into forensic quasi-cross examination of local people who are exercising their democratic right in relation to licensed premises in the vicinity of where they reside, does not always look good and may prove counterproductive. Avoid, unless there is a compelling reason not to do so.

Then it is the turn of the licence holder to set their case out, having heard what all the other parties have to say. Everyone will have their own approach, and it will of course depend on the number of representations, but the focus in most instances should certainly be as much as anything else on the remedial steps that have been taken, or are proposed, by the licence holder. If there is a new proposed DPS then it is advisable that they are in attendance, and where it will assist their CV should have been submitted as part of the supporting evidence on behalf of the licence holder.

It should never be forgotten to express any sadness or even regret at what happened at the premises to cause the Summary Review application in the first place and if any other material matters have been raised by the representations upon the Summary Review then of course they should be addressed. The licence holder (as with every other party) should not forget to point out what they are seeking from the hearing in terms of a determination, including, crucially, in respect of the Interim Step. Whilst all the parties should be reminded of this point by the legal adviser before they make their closing statements, the licence holder should make this point about the full review and the interim steps at this stage in order to set their position out at the earliest available stage.

If a party is asking for the revocation of the licence, then the licence holder certainly needs to address that in their submissions and give the reasons why that is not an appropriate or proportionate step.

It is important that each party is given the opportunity to make representations in respect of both 53C and 53D and as indicated above this is usually expressly provided at the time of closing submissions. Any party who is asking for the licence to be revoked will inevitably submit that the suspension of the licence needs to remain in place, assuming it still is at that stage – it would not be rational for them to assume any other position.

At the end of the hearing the Licensing Subcommittee will retire to make their determination. The Guidance provides for this part of the process as follows:

> ***Determining actions that are appropriate for the promotion of the licensing objectives***
>
> *9.42 Licensing authorities are best placed to determine what actions are appropriate for the promotion of the licensing objectives in their areas. All licensing determinations should be considered on a case-by-case basis. They should take into account any representations or objections that have been received from responsible authorities or other persons, and representations made by the applicant or premises user as the case may be.*

> *9.43 The authority's determination should be evidence-based, justified as being appropriate for the promotion of the licensing objectives and proportionate to what it is intended to achieve.*
>
> *9.44 Determination of whether an action or step is appropriate for the promotion of the licensing objectives requires an assessment of what action or step would be suitable to achieve that end. While this does not therefore require a licensing authority to decide that no lesser step will achieve the aim, the authority should aim to consider the This potential burden that any condition would impose on the premises licence holder (such as the financial burden due to restrictions on licensable activities) as well as the potential benefit in terms of the promotion of the licensing objectives. However, it is imperative that the authority ensures that the factors which form the basis of its determination are limited to consideration of the promotion of the objectives and nothing outside those parameters. As with the consideration of licence variations, the licensing authority should consider wider issues such as other conditions already in place to mitigate potential negative impact on the promotion of the licensing objectives and the track record of the business. Further advice on determining what is appropriate when imposing conditions on a licence or certificate is provided in Chapter 10. The licensing authority is expected to come to its determination based on an assessment of the evidence on both the risks and benefits either for or against making the determination.*

There has been an increasing trend in recent years which arose as a consequence of Covid for decisions under the Act to be communicated five working days after the hearing,[37] but given the strict time limits imposed in relation to Summary Reviews this convention does not apply

[37] Regulation 26(2) Licensing Act 2003 (Hearings) Regulations 2005

here and the deliberation is likely to take place whilst the parties wait, and eventually receive it once it has been arrived at.

Once it has been delivered orally here is then a requirement that the decision is given in writing:

> *(10) Where a relevant licensing authority determines a review under this section it must notify the determination and its reasons for making it to—*
>
> *(a) the holder of the premises licence,*
>
> *(b) any person who made relevant representations, and*
>
> *(c) the chief officer of police for the police area in which the premises are situated (or for each police area in which they are partly situated).*

Each of the decisions under section 53C and 53D takes effect at different times; under section 53C it does not have effect until the end of the period given for appealing against the decision, namely 21 days, or if the decision is appealed against, the time the appeal is disposed of.[38]

The different timings in relation to the decision under section 53D is provided for under subsection 53D(4):

> *(4) Any interim steps taken under subsection (3) apply until—*
>
> *(a) the end of the period given for appealing against a decision made under section 53C,*
>
> *(b) if the decision under section 53C is appealed against, the time the appeal is disposed of, or*

[38] Section 53C(11) Licensing Act 2003

> *(c) the end of a period determined by the relevant licensing authority (which may not be longer than the period of time for which such interim steps could apply under paragraph (a) or (b)).*
>
> *Subsection 53D(4)(c) can be deployed by licence holders in circumstances where they are submitting that the period of the suspension is extended for a short period in order that such matters of staff training can be undertaken prior to reopening.*

The interaction of those two decisions under sections 53C and 53D is provided for in the Guidance:

Review of the interim steps under section 53D

> *12.29 The licensing authority's determination does not have effect until the end of the 21 day period given for appealing the decision, or until the disposal of any appeal that is lodged (see below information on right of appeal). To ensure that there are appropriate and proportionate safeguards in place at all times, the licensing authority is required to review any interim steps that it has taken that are in place on the date of the hearing and consider whether it is appropriate for the promotion of the licensing objectives for the steps to remain in place, or if they should be modified or withdrawn. The review of the interim steps should take place immediately after the determination under section 53C has been reached. In making its decision, the licensing authority must consider any relevant representations made.*
>
> *12.33 The decision of the licensing authority, following the review hearing, will not have effect until the end of the period allowed for appeal, or until the disposal of the appeal.*

As is the differential between the two decisions taking effect:

12.30 In conducting the review of the interim steps the licensing authority has the power to take any of the steps that were available to it at the initial stage (see paragraph 12.13). Any interim steps taken at the review hearing apply until— (a) the end of the period given for appealing against a decision made under section 53C (21 days), (b) if the decision under section 53C is appealed against, the time the appeal is disposed of, or (c) the end of a period determined by the relevant licensing authority (which may not be longer than the period of time for which such interim steps could apply under (a) or (b) above).

CHAPTER EIGHT

APPEALS

Appeals under the Act are provided for in section 181 and Schedule 5. The overarching principle of all such appeals is provided for in section 181:

181 Appeals against decisions of licensing authorities

> *(1) Schedule 5 (which makes provision for appeals against decisions of licensing authorities) has effect.*
>
> *(2) On an appeal in accordance with that Schedule against a decision of a licensing authority, a magistrates' court may—*
>
> *(a) dismiss the appeal,*
>
> *(b) substitute for the decision appealed against any other decision which could have been made by the licensing authority, or*
>
> *(c) remit the case to the licensing authority to dispose of it in accordance with the direction of the court,*
>
> *and may make such order as to costs as it thinks fit.*

Remittance under section 181(2)(c) is a rarely used power and would usually be exercised where the court finds there has been a procedural irregularity performed by the council,[39] and/or when the court wished the local authority to do something outside the scope of the powers that

[39] R (on the application of Hope, Glory Public House Ltd) v City of Westminster Magistrates' Court [2011] EWCA Civ 31

are available to it under section 181(2)(b), and which are of an administrative nature.

In the vast majority of instances any appeal will be allowed under section 181(2)(b) or dismissed under section 181(2)(a).

The majority of appeals following a Summary Review will be against a revocation under section 53C(3)(e) and the maintenance of the suspension of the Premises Licence under section 53D(3)(d), but there can be other combinations and each of those steps act in very different ways but in a way that interacts with the other on a case by case basis.

The period given for all appeals, and where the appeal should be made under the Act is provided for in paragraph 9(1) of Schedule 5 of the Act

> *9(1) An appeal under this Part must be made to a magistrates' court.*
>
> *(2) An appeal under this Part must be commenced by notice of appeal given by the appellant to the designated officer for the magistrates' court within the period of 21 days beginning with the day on which the appellant was notified by the licensing authority of the decision appealed against.*

This point is also dealt with in the Guidance:

> *12.32 An appeal against the final review decision may be made to a magistrates' court within 21 days of the appellant being notified of the licensing authority's determination on the review. An appeal may be made by the premises licence holder, the chief officer of police and/or any other person who made relevant representations.*

As previously identified, the decision (and therefore the 21 days) doesn't commence until it is given in writing and please note carefully that the first day of the 21 is the date it was received, not the following day as with certain civil disputes.

Whilst many decision notices will identify the local Magistrates' Court where an appeal against that Licensing Authority should be made, or filed, this is not enforceable in any way and there is no restriction as to which Magistrates' Court the appeal should be filed at.

This appeal can be filed by posting or hand delivering (good luck finding a member of the court administrative staff to hand it to!) or via email. The latter of those options has to be the most effective, quickest and readily provable method of service.

Each Magistrates' Court's email address is readily available online, sometimes under enquiries@ and listings@ and more recently a central email address has been set up: contactcrime@justice.gov.uk. There is no reason all of these addresses shouldn't be included in the email filing the appeal with the court.

There is a tendency for any appeal against a decision against a Standard Review made under section 52(4) of the Act to file that appeal towards the end of the appeal period for tactical reasons but this is because the decision doesn't take effect during the 21 day appeal period, and if the decision is appealed against, until the appeal is disposed of (as with section 53C) however the coexistence of section 53D means in instances where the suspension of the Premises Licence is maintained and the licence ineffectual, there is no discernible tactical advantage to engaging in such a delay. This is in part because of the insertion of paragraph 8B to Schedule of the Act on 31st January 2017 by the Policing and Crime Act 2017, and in particular Subparagraph 8B(3):

> *8B(1) This paragraph applies where a review of interim steps is decided under section 53D (review of interim steps at a summary review of a premises licence).*
>
> *(2) An appeal may be made against that decision by—*

> *(a) the chief officer of police for the police area (or each police area) in which the premises are situated, or*
>
> *(b) the holder of the premises licence.*
>
> *(3) An appeal under this paragraph must be heard by the magistrates' court within the period of 28 days beginning with the day on which the appellant commenced the appeal (see paragraph 9(2)).*

Prior to this provision being inserted into Schedule 5 there was no requirement for the appeal against interim steps to be heard within a particular time frame and the effect of this was that most licensed businesses that had been subject to a Summary Review where the Premises Licence had been revoked and the suspension of the licence had been maintained, with rent and bills to pay, simply wouldn't make it to the contested hearing as the business would fail beforehand, unless the operator had especially deep pockets, as the appeal would sometimes be over twelve months from the date of the local authority's decision and the licence would be suspended throughout that period. The licensed trade lobbied the government about this gross injustice and accordingly paragraph 8B was inserted into the Act.

It is important to note that these are two separate appeals and to avoid any confusion there should be two separate Notices of Appeal. This will, most likely, mean two separate (and modest) court fees.[40] There is no Magistrates' Court authority to suggest that the court fee needs to be paid within the 21 days and due to an absence of any online means to do so, and a lack of staff to take the payment means this often proves impossible to complete within that timeframe in any event, especially as those staff only tend to work office hours, Monday to Friday. PBA accounts can be used in the Magistrates' Court.

---

40 The Magistrates' Courts Fees Order 2008

Below is a template for an appeal against a decision under section 53C(3):

IN THE [ ] MAGISTRATES' COURT

[ ]

Appellant

and

[COUNCIL]

Respondent

NOTICE OF APPEAL UNDER PART 1 SCHEDULE 5 OF THE LICENSING ACT 2003

[ ], ('the Appellant') premises licence holder, Licence Number: [ ] ('the Licence') at [ ] gives notice of their intention to appeal the decision of the Licensing Subcommittee of [Council] ('the Respondent') following a hearing on [ ], notified by decision notice dated [ ], to revoke the Licence under section 53C(3)(e) of the Licensing Act 2003 (the Act').

The grounds of the appeal are that the decision of the Sub-Committee to revoke the Licence was wrong. Without prejudice to any arguments that may be advanced in due course at the hearing of the appeal, which is heard on a 'de novo' basis, the Appellant contends that the decision of the Sub-Committee was wrong for the following reasons:

[insert grounds]

Signed

....

[name]

[date]

Below is a template for an appeal against a decision under section 53D(3):

IN THE [ ] MAGISTRATES' COURT

[ ]

Appellant

and

[COUNCIL]

Respondent

NOTICE OF APPEAL UNDER PART 1 SCHEDULE 5 OF THE LICENSING ACT 2003

[ ], ('the Appellant') premises licence holder, Licence Number: [ ] ('the Licence') at [ ] gives notice of their intention to appeal the decision of the Licensing Subcommittee of [Council] ('the Respondent') following a hearing on [ ], notified by decision notice dated [ ], to maintain the suspension of the Licence under section 53D(3)(d) of the Licensing Act 2003 (the Act').

The Appellant gives further notice that under Schedule 5, Part 1, Paragraph 8B(3) of the Act, that these appeals under Schedule 5, Part 1, Paragraph 8B(2)(b) of the Act must be heard by the magistrates' court within the period of 28 days beginning with the day of filing this Notice of Appeal.

The grounds of the appeal are that the decision of the Sub-Committee to maintain the suspension of the Licence was wrong. Without prejudice to any arguments that may be advanced in due course at the hearing of the appeal, which is heard on a 'de novo' basis, the Appellant contends that the decision of the Sub-Committee was wrong for the following reasons:

[insert grounds]

Signed

....

[name]

[date]

The bolded and underlined part in the above 53D(3) Notice of Appeal is to draw the court staff's attention to the statutory requirement to hear the appeal within 28 days. The term 'heard' does not provide complete clarity and there are conflicting views on this. To some, it unequivocally means that the substantive appeal is heard and determined within those 28 days, to others it is interpreted that it is listed for (directions) hearing within those 28 days. Given that paragraph was plainly inserted for the benefit of licence holders, a sensible and fair interpretation of that paragraph may be that provision can be interpreted flexibly to the wishes of the licence holder in each particular case. There may be reasons why a small delay beyond the 28 days may be acceptable or even preferable to the licence holder, for reason of evidence gathering or in order to secure a suitable DPS, but certainly if the licence holder wishes the matter to be determined by the court within those 28 days then this is something that should be accommodated by the court and should be robustly requested as such of the court by the licence holding appellant.

The Guidance states that the appeal should be 'heard in full' within 28 days:

Right of appeal against review of interim steps decision

> *12.31 The licence holder or the chief officer of police may appeal against the decision made by the licensing authority concerning its review of the interim steps to a magistrates' court. The appeal must be made within 21 days of the appellant being notified of the licensing authority's decision and* ***must be heard in full by the magistrates' court within 28 days beginning with the day on which the appellant lodged the appeal****. Right of appeal against final review decision.*
> [**emphasis added**]

However, it is difficult to see what force statutory guidance has upon what is ultimately an administrative listing matter for the court.

Whist the Guidance does suggest that both appeals can be heard together:

> *12.34 Where appeals are lodged both against the decision following the review of the interim steps and against the final determination, the courts may decide to consider the appeal against the final determination within the 28 day period, allowing the interim steps appeal to be disposed of at the same time.*

This will rarely be possible (or even desirable for the licence holder) within 28 days.

It is also worth highlighting that should an appeal against the interim step of suspension be allowed and the premises lawfully be permitted to recommence licensable activities, then assuming the period between this and the final, contested appeal passes off significantly without incident then this is likely to make the council amenable to setting the section 53C(3) appeal with the licence holder. Councils are reluctant to go behind the determination of a court and the allowing of an appeal against the maintenance of a suspension, simply put, is the court stating that this licence holder deserves an opportunity to prove themselves based on their proposed steps, and if that opportunity is not spurned by the licence holder then it would be a brave council that contested the appeal against revocation.

In terms of the legal principles involved in the appeals they are the same as in other appeals under the Act and in brief terms are as follows:

- Section 4(3) of the Act states that in carrying out its licensing functions, a licensing authority must also have regard to:

    - *its licensing statement published under section 5, and*

    - *any guidance issued by the Secretary of State under section 182*

  and the court, standing in the shoes of the licensing authority, should follow the same approach

- Any decision arrived at by the Court in an appeal under the Act should promote the Licensing Objectives in a way that is proportionate and balances them against the legitimate business interests of licence holders:

  > *"Licensing decisions often involve weighing a variety of competing considerations: the demand for licensed establishments, the economic benefit to the proprietor and to the locality by drawing in visitors and stimulating the demand, the effect on law and order, the impact on the lives of those who live and work in the vicinity, and so on."* **R (Hope and Glory Public House Limited) v City of Westminster Magistrates' Court [2011] EWCA Civ 31**.

This principle was bolstered by the insertion of paragraph 1.18 into the Guidance in February 2026:

> *1.18 When making licensing decisions, all licensing authorities should consider the need to promote growth and deliver economic benefits.*

- The appeal proceedings are neither criminal nor civil; they require the Court, standing in the shoes of the Respondent's Licensing Subcommittee, to make a proportionate and appropriate determination via the promotion of the four Licensing Objectives.

- Neither the civil nor criminal rules of evidence apply. Licensing appeals are *sui generis*. The Magistrates' Court Rules 1981 provide some assistance in respect of procedural matters in licensing appeals. The Court has a wide discretion as to what evidence it admits, the format in which it is admitted, and the weight it may determine to attach to it. In **Kavanagh v Chief Constable of Devon and Cornwall [1974] 2 All ER 697, CA** on the question of how an appeal hearing should be conducted and what evidence may be called, Lord Denning stated:

  > *"I think they [the Crown Court] should act on the same lines as any administrative body which is charged with an inquiry. They may receive any material which is logically probative even though it is not evidence in a court of law. Hearsay can be permitted where it can fairly be regarded as reliable. No doubt they must act fairly. They should give the party concerned an opportunity of correcting or contradicting what is put against him."*

- The Magistrates' Court on appeal may also properly receive evidence of events that have occurred since the review hearing (**Rushmore Borough Council v Richards [1996] COD 313**.)

- The appeal is neither a complete rehearing "*de novo*", nor entirely a review of the earlier decision. The Court of Appeal provided authoritative guidance on the approach that the Magistrates' Court should take on licensing appeals in the case of **R (Hope and Glory Public House Limited) v City of Westminster Magistrates' Court [2011] EWCA Civ 31**. The case is authority for the following propositions:

    (i) The Court must determine the weight to be attached to the Licensing Subcommittee's decision.

    (ii) The appeal court must determine whether or not the Licensing Subcommittee's decision "is wrong" as at the time of the appeal hearing – even if it was not wrong at the time the decision was made.

    (iii) The onus is on the Appellant to persuade the court that the Licensing Subcommittee should not have exercised its discretion in the way it did, based on the evidence before the Court at the time of the appeal hearing.

- In reaching its decision the Magistrates' Court should consider:

    i. The statutory function to determine an application for a review of a premises licence pursuant to section 53A of the Act.

    ii. The relevant parts of the Guidance, especially Part 12 on Summary Reviews.

    iii. The council's Statement of Licensing Policy.

    iv. The evidence before the Licensing Subcommittee, and what evidence it considered and what it did not.

v. Updated and new evidence presented in the appeal by both parties in writing and orally, importantly and distinguishable from the review hearing, tested before a Court.

vi. The decision of the Licensing Subcommittee, its written reasons, and the weight the Court decides to attach to it, in light of any new evidence, before it determines whether the decision was wrong.

Summary

Behind the sections inserted after the Act came into force are stories replete with greater drama and tragedy than any others in the world of licencing. They can involve loss of life and loss of livelihood, but the former, tragic as it is, does not mean that the latter is inevitable.

The event that gives rise to the Summary Review in the first place is a hugely important component, but the conduct of the premises on the night in question, and their dealing with responsible authorities in the aftermath will usually define the direction of travel to an even greater extent, especially if the premises in question has a previously uneventful track record.

It is hoped that this book will prove a useful tool for anyone involved in this structured, but fast moving regulatory process and that it will enable licence holders in particular to take the appropriate steps, at the correct time, and in the correct way retain their business at the end of the Summary Review.

MORE BOOKS BY LAW BRIEF PUBLISHING

A selection of our other titles available now:-

'A Practical Guide to Probation Breaches and Other Applications' by Mark Thomas
'A Practical Guide to Remarriage and Divorce' by Cordelia Williams & Claire Howard
'A Practical Guide to Privacy, Transparency, Reporting Restrictions and Closed Proceedings in the Court of Protection' by Laura Mannering
'Beaumont on Barristers – A Guide to Defending Disciplinary Proceedings (Second Edition)' by Marc Beaumont
'A Practical Guide to Payments for Environmental Services' by Ben Sharples
'A Practical Guide to the Law of Pregnancy and Maternity at Work' by Rebecca Thomas
'A Practical Guide to Redundancy – Second Edition' by Philip Hyland & Collette Moore
'A Practical Guide to International Issues for Scottish Family Lawyers' by Susie Mountain, Donna McKay, Ken MacDonald
'A Practical Guide to the Law on Deprivation of Liberty' by Ben Troke
'A Practical Guide to Rights over Airspace and Subsoil – Second Edition' by Daniel Gatty
'A Practical Guide to the Law in Relation to Inquests' by Ramya Nagesh
'A Practical Guide to the Construction and Rectification of Wills and Trust Instruments (Second Edition)' by Edward Hewitt
'A Practical Guide to Data Protection in Social Housing' by Clare Paterson
'A Practical Guide to Spousal Maintenance – Second Edition' by Liz Cowell
'A Practical Guide to International Parental Child Abduction Law (England and Wales)' by Dr Onyója Momoh
'A Practical Guide to Deprivation of British Citizenship' by Sean Ell
'A Practical Guide to Commercial Property Service Charges' by Rachel Garton
'A Practical Guide to Clinical Negligence – Third Edition' by Geoffrey Simpson-Scott (Geoff)
'A Practical Guide to the Rights of Grandparents in Children Proceedings – Second Edition' by Stuart Barlow

'The Electronic Communications Code: A Practical Guide – Second Edition' by Kerry Bretherton KC, James Castle, Mark Loveday

'A Practical Guide to the Independent School Standards – September 2023 Edition' by Sarah McKimm

'A Practical Guide to Estate Administration and Crypto Assets' by Richard Marshall

'A Practical Guide to Parental Alienation in Private and Public Law Children Cases' by Sam King QC & Frankie Shama

'Contested Heritage – Removing Art from Land and Historic Buildings' by Richard Harwood QC, Catherine Dobson, David Sawtell

'The Limits of Separate Legal Personality: When Those Running a Company Can Be Held Personally Liable for Losses Caused to Third Parties Outside of the Company' by Dr Mike Wilkinson

'A Practical Guide to Transgender Law' by Robin Moira White & Nicola Newbegin

'A Practical Guide to 'Stranded Spouses' in Family Law' by Mani Singh Basi

'A Practical Guide to Residential Freehold Conveyancing' by Lorraine Richardson

'A Practical Guide to Pensions on Divorce for Lawyers' by Bryan Scant

'A Practical Guide to Challenging Sham Marriage Allegations in Immigration Law' by Priya Solanki

'A Practical Guide to Digital Communications Evidence in Criminal Law' by Sam Willis

'A Practical Guide to Legal Rights in Scotland' by Sarah-Jane Macdonald

'A Practical Guide to New Build Conveyancing' by Paul Sams & Rebecca East

'A Practical Guide to Inherited Wealth on Divorce' by Hayley Trim

'A Practical Guide to Practice Direction 12J and Domestic Abuse in Private Law Children Proceedings' by Rebecca Cross & Malvika Jaganmohan

'A Practical Guide to Confiscation and Restraint' by Narita Bahra QC, John Carl Townsend, David Winch

'A Practical Guide to the Law of Forests in Scotland' by Philip Buchan

'A Practical Guide to Health and Medical Cases in Immigration Law' by Rebecca Chapman & Miranda Butler

'A Practical Guide to Bad Character Evidence for Criminal Practitioners by Aparna Rao

'A Practical Guide to Extradition Law post-Brexit' by Myles Grandison et al

'A Practical Guide to Hoarding and Mental Health for Housing Lawyers' by Rachel Coyle

'Stephens on Contractual Indemnities' by Richard Stephens
'A Practical Guide to the EU Succession Regulation' by Richard Frimston
'A Practical Guide to Solicitor and Client Costs – Second Edition' by Robin Dunne
'Constructive Dismissal – Practice Pointers and Principles' by Benjimin Burgher
'A Practical Guide to Religion and Belief Discrimination Claims in the Workplace' by Kashif Ali
'A Practical Guide to the Law of Medical Treatment Decisions' by Ben Troke
'Fundamental Dishonesty and QOCS in Personal Injury Proceedings: Law and Practice' by Jake Rowley
'A Practical Guide to the Law in Relation to School Exclusions' by Charlotte Hadfield & Alice de Coverley
'A Practical Guide to Divorce for the Silver Separators' by Karin Walker
'The Right to be Forgotten – The Law and Practical Issues' by Melissa Stock
'A Practical Guide to Planning Law and Rights of Way in National Parks, the Broads and AONBs' by James Maurici QC, James Neill et al
'A Practical Guide to Election Law' by Tom Tabori
'A Practical Guide to the Law in Relation to Surrogacy' by Andrew Powell
'A Practical Guide to Claims Arising from Fatal Accidents – Second Edition' by James Patience
'A Practical Guide to Asbestos Claims' by Jonathan Owen & Gareth McAloon
'A Practical Guide to Stamp Duty Land Tax in England and Northern Ireland' by Suzanne O'Hara
'A Practical Guide to the Law of Farming Partnerships' by Philip Whitcomb
'A Practical Guide to the Law of Unlawful Eviction and Harassment – Second Edition' by Stephanie Lovegrove
'A Practical Guide to Costs in Personal Injury Claims – Second Edition' by Matthew Hoe
'A Practical Guide to the General Data Protection Regulation (GDPR) – Second Edition' by Keith Markham
'A Practical Guide to Working with Litigants in Person and McKenzie Friends in Family Cases' by Stuart Barlow
'Protecting Unregistered Brands: A Practical Guide to the Law of Passing Off' by Lorna Brazell
'A Practical Guide to Secondary Liability and Joint Enterprise Post-Jogee' by Joanne Cecil & James Mehigan

‘A Practical Guide to the Pre-Action RTA Claims Protocol for Personal Injury Lawyers’ by Antonia Ford
‘A Practical Guide to Neighbour Disputes and the Law’ by Alexander Walsh
‘A Practical Guide to Coercive Control for Legal Practitioners and Victims’ by Rachel Horman
‘A Practical Guide to the Law of Driverless Cars – Second Edition’
by Alex Glassbrook, Emma Northey & Scarlett Milligan
‘A Practical Guide to TOLATA Claims’ by Greg Williams
‘A Practical Guide to Elderly Law – Second Edition’ by Justin Patten
‘A Practical Guide to Responding to Housing Disrepair and Unfitness Claims’ by Iain Wightwick
‘A Practical Guide to the Law of Bullying and Harassment in the Workplace’ by Philip Hyland
‘How to Be a Freelance Solicitor: A Practical Guide to the SRA-Regulated Freelance Solicitor Model’ by Paul Bennett
‘A Practical Guide to Prison Injury Claims’ by Malcolm Johnson
‘A Practical Guide to Advising Clients at the Police Station’ by Colin Stephen McKeown-Beaumont
‘A Practical Guide to Antisocial Behaviour Injunctions – Second Edition’ by Iain Wightwick
‘Practical Mediation: A Guide for Mediators, Advocates, Advisers, Lawyers, and Students in Civil, Commercial, Business, Property, Workplace, and Employment Cases’ by Jonathan Dingle with John Sephton
‘The Mini-Pupillage Workbook’ by David Boyle
‘A Practical Guide to Crofting Law’ by Brian Inkster
‘A Practical Guide to the Law of Domain Names and Cybersquatting’ by Andrew Clemson
‘A Practical Guide to the Law of Gender Pay Gap Reporting’ by Harini Iyengar
‘NHS Whistleblowing and the Law’ by Joseph England
‘Employment Law and the Gig Economy’ by Nigel Mackay & Annie Powell
‘A Practical Guide to Noise Induced Hearing Loss (NIHL) Claims’ by Andrew Mckie, Ian Skeate, Gareth McAloon
‘An Introduction to Beauty Negligence Claims – A Practical Guide for the Personal Injury Practitioner’ by Greg Almond
‘Intercompany Agreements for Transfer Pricing Compliance’ by Paul Sutton
‘Zen and the Art of Mediation’ by Martin Plowman
‘A Practical Guide to Adoption for Family Lawyers’ by Graham Pegg

'A Practical Guide to Industrial Disease Claims' by Andrew Mckie & Ian Skeate
'A Practical Guide to Conducting a Sheriff Court Proof' by Andrew Stevenson
'A Practical Guide to Vicarious Liability' by Mariel Irvine
'A Practical Guide to Applications for Landlord's Consent and Variation of Leases' by Mark Shelton
'A Practical Guide to Relief from Sanctions Post-Mitchell and Denton' by Peter Causton
'A Practical Guide to Equity Release for Advisors' by Paul Sams
'A Practical Guide to Financial Services Claims' by Chris Hegarty
'A Practical Guide to Financial Ombudsman Service Claims' by Adam Temple & Robert Scrivenor
'A Practical Guide to Running Housing Disrepair and Cavity Wall Claims – Second Edition' by Andrew Mckie & Ian Skeate
'A Practical Guide to Holiday Sickness Claims – Second Edition' by Andrew Mckie & Ian Skeate
'Arguments and Tactics for Personal Injury and Clinical Negligence Claims' by Dorian Williams
'A Practical Guide to Drone Law' by Rufus Ballaster, Andrew Firman, Eleanor Clot
'On Experts: CPR35 for Lawyers and Experts' by David Boyle
'An Introduction to Personal Injury Law' by David Boyle

www.ingramcontent.com/pod-product-compliance
Lightning Source LLC
LaVergne TN
LVHW022101200926
848481LV00003B/1027